The
Man Who
Quit
Money

Also By Mark Sundeen

Car Camping
The Making of Toro
North by Northwestern
(with Captain Sig Hansen)

The
Man Who
Quit
Money

. . .

MARK SUNDEEN

Riverhead Books
New York

RIVERHEAD BOOKS
Published by the Penguin Group
Penguin Group (USA) Inc.
375 Hudson Street, New York, New York 10014, USA
Penguin Group (Canada), 90 Eglinton Avenue East, Suite 700, Toronto, Ontario M4P 2Y3, Canada
(a division of Pearson Penguin Canada Inc.)
Penguin Books Ltd., 80 Strand, London WC2R 0RL, England
Penguin Group Ireland, 25 St. Stephen's Green, Dublin 2, Ireland (a division of Penguin Books Ltd.)
Penguin Group (Australia), 250 Camberwell Road, Camberwell, Victoria 3124, Australia
(a division of Pearson Australia Group Pty. Ltd.)
Penguin Books India Pvt. Ltd., 11 Community Centre, Panchsheel Park, New Delhi—110 017,
India
Penguin Group (NZ), 67 Apollo Drive, Rosedale, Auckland 0632, New Zealand
(a division of Pearson New Zealand Ltd.)
Penguin Books (South Africa) (Pty.) Ltd., 24 Sturdee Avenue, Rosebank, Johannesburg 2196,
South Africa

Penguin Books Ltd., Registered Offices: 80 Strand, London WC2R 0RL, England

The publisher does not have any control over and does not assume any responsibility for author or
third-party websites or their content.

First Riverhead trade paperback edition: March 2012

Library of Congress Cataloging-in-Publication Data

Sundeen, Mark, date.
 The man who quit money / Mark Sundeen.
  p. cm.
 ISBN 978-1-59448-569-5
 1. Suelo, Daniel. 2. Self-reliant living—United States. 3. Alternative lifestyles—United
States. 4. Money—Social aspects. 5. Simplicity. I. Title.
 CT275.S87445S86 2011
 332.4'9792092—dc23
 [B]

                                                                            2011049882

PRINTED IN THE UNITED STATES OF AMERICA

20   19   18   17   16   15   14   13

For Cedar,
who gave me the kernels anyway

Do not worry about your life, what you will eat or drink; or about your body, what you will wear. Is not life more important than food, and the body more important than clothes? Look at the birds of the air; they do not sow or reap or store away in the barns, and yet your heavenly Father feeds them ... Who of you by worrying can add a single hour to his life?

—**Jesus**

Let us live happily, then, though we call nothing our own! We shall be like the bright gods, feeding on happiness!

—**Buddha**

Home is anywhere I'm living, if it's sleeping on some vacant bench in City Square.

—**Merle Haggard**

The
Man Who
Quit
Money

Part One

1

. . .

IN THE FIRST year of the twenty-first century, a man standing by a highway in the middle of America pulled from his pocket his life savings—thirty dollars—laid it inside a phone booth, and walked away. He was thirty-nine years old, came from a good family, and had been to college. He was not mentally ill, nor an addict. His decision appears to have been an act of free will by a competent adult.

In the twelve years since, as the Dow Jones skyrocketed to its all-time high, Daniel Suelo has not earned, received, or spent a single dollar. In an era when anyone who could sign his name qualified for a mortgage, Suelo did not apply for loans or write IOUs. He didn't even barter. As the public debt soared to eight, ten, finally thirteen trillion dollars, he did not pay taxes, or accept food stamps, welfare, or any other form of government handout.

Instead he set up house in caves in the Utah canyonlands,

where he forages mulberries and wild onions, scavenges roadkill raccoons and squirrels, pulls expired groceries from dumpsters, and is often fed by friends and strangers. "My philosophy is to use only what is freely given or discarded & what is already present & already running," he writes. While the rest of us grapple with tax deductions, variable-rate mortgages, retirement plans, and money-market accounts, Suelo no longer holds so much as an identification card.

Yet the man who sleeps under bridges and prospects in trash cans is not a typical hobo. He does not panhandle, and he often works—declining payment for his efforts. While he is driven by spiritual beliefs and longings, he is not a monk, nor is he associated with any church. And although he lives in a cave, he is not a hermit: he is relentlessly social, remains close with friends and family, and engages in discussions with strangers via the website he maintains from the public library. He has crisscrossed the West by bicycle, hopped freight trains, hitched through nearly every state in the union, hauled nets on a Bering Sea trawler, harvested mussels and kelp from Pacific beaches, spearfished salmon in Alaska streams, and braved three months of storms atop an ancient hemlock tree.

"I know it is possible to live with zero money," Suelo declares. "Abundantly."

. . .

As it happens, I had met Suelo long before he gave up money, in the desert outpost of Moab, Utah, a haven for seekers and dropouts. We ran in the same circle, worked a stint together as cooks, and squatted on public lands, not as a statement against something, but because we didn't want to pay rent. We had both gone truant from career paths because we were angry about the way the world was, and had no means of changing it. If we couldn't overthrow the bastards, then at least we wouldn't enter data in their cubicles and buy junk in their big boxes and make payments on their LandCrunchers. But over the years, we drifted our separate ways, geographically and otherwise.

By the time I set out to find him again, we hadn't had a conversation in more than a decade. I had heard of Daniel's attempt to live without money, and I'd assumed he had simply lost his mind. For my part, I was no longer an itinerant river guide living in my truck on eight thousand a year, but a professional writer now and then passing through town to pull weeds and repair the plumbing at my rental property, a trailer on an acre of tumbleweeds whose market value had tripled in three years, thank you very much. My one connection to the cave dweller was that he had friended me on Facebook.

I'd seen him once in the intervening years, though. On a visit to Moab, I had glanced at a shaggy gray-haired man across the aisle at the market. We made tentative eye contact. He looked familiar, but could this old guy, gray in the muzzle, with deep lines on his face and pants worn thin, be the Daniel I had cooked with a decade before?

He smiled at me. The sight of his teeth, dark and crooked, rotting right there in his mouth—it chilled me. As much as I supported a person's right to voluntary poverty, here at the height of America's greatest prosperity, I drew the line at bad teeth. I should not be forced to look at such a sorry mouth. The sight made me ashamed—of my own excellent dental condition, my disposable income, my rental property—as if he had accused me directly. My shame made me mad. It was a free country, I conceded, and Suelo had every right to sleep in the dirt and lasso grasshoppers or whatever, but how dare he sit in judgment of me?

By now I had recognized my old acquaintance beyond doubt. But I did not take his hand, offer my friendship, ask about his health. I didn't even say hello. My jaw tightening, I threw him a nod and escaped to my car.

The truth was, I'd come to *like* money. In fact, I had always liked it. When I was a boy, I counted and recounted the coins I collected in a tin can, packing pennies and nickels into paper rolls and depositing them at the bank, greatly satisfied as my fortune grew on the passbook. I also liked what money represented, the entire system of trade and credit and saving. As I grew up, money served me well: I started getting paid to do what I wanted, like writing books. Money allowed me to test my wits, to save, to gamble, to win. Even in my days of living in a tent, the act of *saving* money allowed me more freedom. And now, when I hunted for a used car below Blue Book value, or refinanced my house at a lower rate, I felt like I'd outwitted the system.

After surviving well into my thirties with only the possessions that could fit inside the bed of a pickup, I began to reap the rewards of my pennies saved and pennies earned. I acquired a second car and a second house (okay, one was that singlewide), contributed to a retirement account, and filed fifty-three pages of tax returns. I possessed six pairs of skis.

Then came 2008. Twenty trillion dollars in world assets were incinerated by bad mortgages and speculation. The real-estate bubble splattered into foreclosure and bankruptcy, taking down with it the pensions and savings and jobs of millions of people. My paltry retirement account became 50 percent paltrier. Magazines that employed me furloughed staff, or shut down altogether.

Budget cuts would eventually eliminate my college teaching job. Suddenly that big monthly payment on my home didn't seem like money well spent. I could paint all I wanted, but no number of trips to Home Depot would make the house worth what I had paid for it. Those naysayers who forecast that my generation, born in the 1960s and 1970s, would be the first in America's history to be worse off than their parents: maybe they had a point.

Suelo meanwhile had gained a little notoriety, thanks to stories in *Details* magazine and the *Denver Post*, an interview with the BBC, even the pages of *Ripley's Believe It or Not*. His blog and website got tens of thousands of hits. As I pored over the writings he had compiled, from Thomas Jefferson and Socrates and Saint Augustine, I began to think about the choices he had made, bad teeth and all. Here was someone who had said all along what the rest of us were being forced to contemplate for the first time, now that our bubble of prosperity had burst: money was an illusion. "I simply got tired of acknowledging as real this most common worldwide belief called money," cried this voice in the desert. "I simply got tired of being unreal."

Daniel had opted out entirely, rejected what I had pursued. I wondered whether, apart from everything he rejected, there was something he embraced. What was I missing out on? Finally I decided to drive to the Utah desert and find out for myself.

·   ·   ·

I RETURNED TO Moab. I was staying with friends, a married couple. I had exchanged a few emails with Suelo, but we had failed to make a foolproof plan. Of course he had no phone. And apart from any question of cave etiquette—was it okay to just drop by?—I didn't know where to locate him in the vast wilderness.

I sent an email, then sat back and hoped that he wandered out of the canyon soon, and logged on at the library.

A day passed. It was fall, and the air was sunny and cool and crisp. I sat on my friends' porch, sipping a glass of fresh watermelon juice. One of my hosts, Melony (her real name, I swear), considered watermelon a wonder food, filled with antioxidants and electrolytes and vitamins. She swore it had cured her of a five-year illness that no doctor, medication, or allergy panels could solve, and she drank the red potion three times a day, stuffing rinds, seeds, and everything into a blender. But with the harvest over, and both markets in town sold out, she was running low. With winter approaching, she was contemplating doing something desperate, like ordering them on the Internet. Another day passed, and still no word from Suelo.

And then, as I sat on the porch checking my watch, an apparition appeared. A bicycle was approaching: dark mount, dark rider. Horn-rimmed glasses emerged between gray hair and beard. The rider wore a black felt bolero cinched under his chin, with a stampede strap held snug by a tin brooch. His gaze was forward, serene. Although his legs were clearly pumping, his body gave the impression of utter calm. As he pedaled toward me I made out a plastic crate of apples and oranges lashed to a rear rack. I would not have been surprised had he let go of the handlebars, plucked the fruit from the basket, and begun to juggle.

I rushed into the street and called, "Daniel!" He slowed to a halt, then turned the bike around and looked at me, puzzled, until I identified myself.

"Oh, it's you," he said.

For a dude who lives in a cave, Suelo displayed a positively keen sense of style. His trousers were a few inches too long, cuffed with rolls above boxy workman shoes. A plaid flannel over a tight black T-shirt revealed a slice of trim belly above a leather belt. He looked like a cross between a Great Depression hobo and a vagabond French painter—Buster Keaton meets Paul Gauguin.

Unsure what to do next, I threw my arms around him in a clumsy hug. He smelled like wood smoke. I invited him inside and introduced him to Melony and her husband, Mathew. Melony poured tall glasses of watermelon juice—the last of her cache, she told us.

Suelo perked up. Above his right eye is a scar that causes the brow to rise in a sharp peak, giving him a perpetual appearance of intense curiosity.

"Do you know about the melon patch?" he said.

We didn't.

"That field between the creeks," he said, nodding toward the street. "There's hundreds of melons over there. Watermelon. Crenshaws. Squash and pumpkins, too. I've been eating them for months."

"Whose are they?" I said.

"Some guy." He shrugged. "After Obama was elected, he thought the whole system would collapse, so he planted his fallow fields. But the end-times didn't come, so he left everything to rot."

Mathew and Melony and I followed Suelo out of the house and onto the street. He pushed his bike along the paved road until it turned to dirt, leading us to a field nestled between two creeks, a green swath of desert farmland that had survived from pioneer days. Someone had planted all kinds of trees and vines that grew out of the ground—trees that were pleasing to the eye and good for food. Peach trees. Pear trees. Apple trees. Only the serpent and the naked lady were missing.

And there were hundreds of melons, a cornucopia, some tucked green into the rows of thistle and tumbleweed, others already yellow mush swelling in the sun. Suelo cradled a sound one like a baby and thwapped it with his thumb.

"If the thud is too deep, it's overripe."

We wandered the rows, tapping and listening.

"Does anyone have a knife?" Melony asked. Suelo had left his on the bike. But no matter. He picked up a melon the size of a pony keg and raised it overhead, then heaved it down. It burst at his feet with a *whump*. He knelt beside it, scooped up the flesh, and lapped it from his palms.

And then, verily, he fed our multitude.

Wordlessly, Mathew and Melony shoveled watermelon into their mouths as the syrup dripped toward their elbows. I buried my face till my nose bumped against rind. We busted melons open, one after another, some putrid, others green, some delectable. It was cool and dry and sunny, and the sandy soil was wet after the first big rain of October. The field was ringed by cottonwoods exploding in yellow, like a million kernels of popcorn. Beyond the trees, the red cliffs bore down, and above them the snowy peaks thrust through a ring of clouds into the blue sky. We all ate and were satisfied. The number of those who ate was four.

"I don't remember the leaves ever being this yellow," Suelo said, drying his wrist on his pants. "Too bad all the squash are rotten."

Looking across the fields, we could see that Mathew and Melony's house stood just a hundred yards away, a literal stone's throw from this Eden. It seemed truly mystical how unfindable, moneyless Suelo had materialized from the ether and led us across the desert, to Melontopia. To the abundance.

Mathew and Melony and I filled our arms with melons, hoarding them like iGadgets we'd liberated from Best Buy after a hurricane. But Suelo chose only a single, small green fruit. He lowered it into his crate and silently pedaled off.

2

. . .

"OUR WHOLE SOCIETY is designed so that you have to have
money," Suelo says. "You have to be a part of the capitalist system. It's illegal to live outside of it."

He has a point. Our national identity is enmeshed with the
idea of private property—our right to it is enshrined in the Fourteenth Amendment, which guarantees that we not be deprived
of it, any more than of our lives or liberty, "without due process
of law." The flip side of this protection of property holders, however, is a lack of protection for the property-less. And nowhere
is this more apparent than with respect to real estate. The American Indian belief that man can no more own land than he can
own air or sunlight was quashed with the arrival of Europe-
ans. The ground beneath their feet was available for the taking,
and over a period of three centuries, white people took it, until
the frontier closed around the year 1900, after which all real
estate in America was spoken for. The legal supremacy of private

property—a relatively recent human invention—is cemented in the American logic, as indisputable as the laws of physics. If you step off the roof, gravity will pull you to the ground. If you don't pay the rent, the landlord will evict you. And if you squat in an abandoned building, you are guilty of trespassing.

Even lands set aside for the public do not welcome a man without money. While a company may drill a mine or erect an oil rig on federal property, a citizen is prohibited from building a cabin there. Homesteading has been outlawed for more than a century. Visitors to national forests must vacate their campsites after fourteen days, and often must pay a nightly fee. Living in city parks and on sidewalks is deemed vagrancy and banned in most places. The punishment for sleeping in an unused public space that requires little upkeep—under a railroad trestle, or along a river—is often to sleep in an expensive jail built with tax dollars.

Suelo has defied these laws. His primary residence is the canyons near Arches National Park, where he has lived in a dozen caves tucked into sandstone nooks. In the fall of 2002, two years after quitting money, he homesteaded a majestic alcove high on a cliff, two hundred feet across and fifty feet tall. Its sculpted mouth was windblown into smooth symmetry. Sitting inside and gazing into the gorge below felt like heralding himself to the world from inside the bell of a trumpet.

Suelo's grotto was a two-hour walk from pavement, and believing he was unlikely to be disturbed, he settled in for the long haul. He chipped at the rocky ground to create a wide, flat bed, and lined it with tarps and pads and sleeping bags that had been left out with someone else's trash. He stacked rocks to block the wind, and built wood-burning cookstoves from old tin cans. He learned to forage for cactus pods, yucca seeds, wildflowers, and the watercress that grew in the creek. From dumpsters he stockpiled dry goods like rice and beans and flour, and sealed them in plastic buckets. He drank from springs, bathed in the creek. He washed his clothing by weighting it overnight with a river rock, dried it on the hot sandstone. He arranged on stone slabs a library of books. From a chunk of talus he carved a statue, a ponderous head like some monolith from Easter Island.

In warm months the cave attracted occasional hikers, and when Suelo was away, he left a note. *Feel free to camp here. What's mine is yours. Eat any of my food. Read my books. Take them with you if you'd like.* Visitors left notes in return, saying they were pleased with his caretaking.

Then one day, after several years of peace, a ranger from the Bureau of Land Management arrived to evict him. Suelo had long since violated the fourteen-day limit.

"If I were hiking along here and I saw this camp," said the ranger, "I'd feel like I wasn't allowed here, that it was someone else's space. But this is public land."

"Are you saying this because you're paid to say it, or because you really believe it?"

"Well, I do have to keep my personal and my professional opinions separated," said the ranger. "But you are making a high impact here."

Suelo said, "Who do you think is making a higher impact on the earth: you or me?"

The ranger wrote a ticket for $120.

"Well, I don't use money," Suelo said. "So I can't pay this."

Not only did he not use money, he had discarded his passport and driver's license. He had even discarded his legal surname, Shellabarger, in favor of Suelo, Spanish for "soil." He chose the name spontaneously, back in his tree-sitting days in Oregon, when he caught sight of a sticker that said ALL SOIL IS SACRED. "Suelo" stuck.

The ranger felt conflicted. He'd spent years chasing vandals and grave robbers through these canyons; he knew that Suelo was not harming the land. In some ways, Suelo was a model steward. The ranger offered to drive him to the next county to see a judge and resolve the citation. The next day, these odd bedfellows, a penniless hobo and a federal law enforcer, climbed into a shimmering government-issue truck and sped across the desert. As they drove, Suelo outlined his philosophy of moneyless living while the ranger explained why he had become a land manager— to stop people from destroying nature. "And then someone like you comes along," he said, "and I struggle with my conscience."

They arrived at the courthouse. The judge was a kindly white-haired man. "So you live without money," he drawled. "This is an honorable thing. But we live in the modern world. We have all these laws for a reason."

Suelo hears this all the time: that we're living in different times now, that however noble his values, their practice is obsolete. He even heard it once when he knocked on the door of a Buddhist monastery and asked to spend the night, and a monk informed him that rates began at fifty dollars.

The Buddha himself would have been turned away, Suelo observed.

"We're living in a different age than the Buddha," he was told.

But Suelo simply doesn't accept this distinction. Whether today or two thousand years ago, he believes, public spaces are for the public, and he need not ask permission to occupy one. When a policeman asks what he's doing as he hitchhikes into town or pulls a pizza from a dumpster, he says, "Walking in America."

"It resonates with cops," Suelo says. "A lot of them are very patriotic, many are veterans, and they understand that every citizen should have the right to walk in this country."

To the Utah judge casting about for an appropriate sentence, Suelo questioned the purpose of the fourteen-day camping limit. "Does it have anything to do with justice or protecting the environment? No. It's to keep people like me from existing." Daniel offered to do jail time or community service.

"I don't think jail would be appropriate," said the judge. Like the ranger, the monk, and the many cops who meet Suelo, the judge just didn't know what to do with someone who refused to abide by one of our culture's most basic premises—the use of currency as a means of exchange. Finally he said, "Well, what do *you* think you should have to do?"

Suelo suggested service at a shelter for abused women and children. They agreed on twenty hours. Suelo volunteered regularly at the shelter anyway, so the punishment was a bit like sending Brer Rabbit back to the briar patch. And within a few weeks of eviction from his grand manor, he found a new cave, this time a tiny crevice where he would not be discovered.

·   ·   ·

It's TEMPTING TO conclude that Suelo's years in the wilderness have transformed him into a crusader for the earth. During his 2001 stint as a tree sitter, he was exactly that. A year after quitting money, he perched atop an Oregon hemlock for three months, alone most of the time, disregarding threats from the sheriff and the buzzing saws of loggers. He and his fellow activists saved the grove from being cut down.

And clearly his lifestyle has a lower impact than virtually anybody else's in America. Without a car or a home to heat and cool, he produces hardly any carbon dioxide. Foraging for wild raspberries and spearfishing salmon has close to zero environmental cost—no production, no transportation. And although food gathered from a dumpster must be grown and processed and shipped, rescuing it from the trash actually prevents the further expenditure of energy to haul and bury that excess in a landfill. Suelo brings into existence no bottles, cans, wrappers, bags, packaging, nor those plastic six-pack rings that you're supposed to snip up with scissors to save the seabirds. As for the benefits of pitching Coke bottles into the recycling bin—Suelo is the guy pulling those bottles *out* of the bin, using them until they crack, then pitching them back. The carbon footprint of the average American is about twenty tons per year. Suelo's output is probably closer to that of an Ethiopian—about two hundred pounds, or about one half of 1 percent of an American's.

"He wants to have the smallest ecological footprint and the largest possible impact at improving the world," says his best friend, Damian Nash. "His life goal since I met him is to take as little and give as much as possible."

Yet saving the earth is not Suelo's primary mission. His energy use before giving up money was already so low that quitting money caused only a negligible decline. And even after his successful tree sit, he questions the value of political action. "I don't know if it does any good. We're feeding the roots and pruning the branches—and they flourish more, actually. If we really want to help, we shouldn't feed the monster in the first place, and that's the monetary system."

.   .   .

SUELO'S QUEST FOR Free Parking might be easy if he availed himself of government programs or private homeless shelters. But Suelo refuses these charities as by-products of the money system he rejects. Government programs are funded by taxes paid not freely but out of legal obligation. Most shelters are staffed by paid workers who "give" only with the expectation of a check.

Suelo does, however, accept hospitality that is freely given. He has knocked on the door of a Catholic Workers house, a Unitarian church, and a Zen center, and has been offered a place to sleep. He has spent time in a number of communes, including one in Georgia where members weave hammocks to provide income, and another in Oregon where residents grow their own vegetables. In Portland, Oregon, he stays at urban squats populated by anarchists, or in communal homes that welcome transients.

Suelo is also welcomed by family, friends, and complete strangers. He has an open invitation to stay with his parents in Grand Junction, Colorado, his brother Doug Shellabarger near Denver, his friend Damian Nash in Moab, and a half-dozen others across the country. Tim Wojtusik, in eastern Oregon, is not surprised when, after no word for months, he wakes to discover his friend camped in the backyard. Suelo has lost count of the times someone picked him up hitchhiking, then brought him home and served him a meal. A Navajo man gave his own bed to Suelo and slept on the couch, then in the morning treated him to breakfast.

Through two decades in Moab, Suelo has developed a reputation as a reliable house sitter. In a town of seasonal workers who often leave home for months at a time, his services are in high demand. He spent one winter hopping from one house-sit to the next. For a time a friend invited him to stay in a tree house in her backyard, until a neighbor complained.

Even with all the roofs offered, Suelo spends the majority of his nights outdoors. He camps in wilderness, the red rock country around Sedona, Arizona, or the Gila of New Mexico, where he spent a few weeks learning survival skills from a hermit. He and some friends rode bikes from Portland to Wyoming, camping along the road. He has hopped trains all across the country. One summer Suelo colonized an island in the Willamette River in the heart of Portland. He commandeered a piece of plastic dock that had floated downstream, and paddled it to the brambles of the undeveloped island. He carved out a clearing in the thick brush so that he couldn't be seen from shore. "I had visions of building a cob house," he says, but that didn't pan out. He spent another summer in the woods by Mount Tamalpais, just north of San Francisco. He dropped his pack just thirty feet from a trail and lived undetected in the heart of one of the wealthiest zip codes in America. He spent a month camped in a bird refuge on the University of Florida campus in Gainesville. Turns out there are plenty of places to sleep free in America: you just have to know where to look.

These days, in addition to the cave, he maintains a camp within Moab city limits, hidden in a thicket on private property. It looks like a typical homeless squat: torn plastic tarps draped over a tent, pots and dishes scattered in the dirt. One morning, the landowner saw smoke from the fire and came running with a shovel and blanket. He was relieved to find that it was just Suelo, whom he'd known for years. The landowner told him not to build fires, and while he didn't exactly grant Suelo permission to stay, he more or less turned a blind eye.

The town camp saves Suelo the two-hour commute to his cave, and sometimes he crashes there after a late night in town. But the truth is, he largely sleeps wherever he chooses to. "I've found you can camp anywhere, as long as you're just a few feet off the pavement," Suelo says. "People don't notice you. I've slept right beside a police station."

. . .

WAIT A MINUTE. Isn't Suelo just kidding himself? Is there really any difference between accepting a room in a church and a room in a homeless shelter? And isn't hitchhiking in a gas-powered automobile or blogging from a library computer evidence that he is just as dependent on money as the rest of us—if not on the green paper itself, then certainly the commerce without which there would be no cars or gasoline or libraries or computers?

Suelo considers these criticisms. He concedes that by using the public library, he is accepting other people's tax money, and for a while considered stopping the practice, accessing the Internet only at friends' houses. But ultimately he felt he was splitting hairs a bit too finely. He certainly wasn't going to stop walking on public roads merely because they were paid for with taxes. Our economic lives are so intertwined that he could never achieve absolute purity. His intention is to give freely what he has without expectation of return, and to accept without obligation that which is freely given by others.

That said, he constantly rethinks and interprets the rules of living without money. After his first couple of months of this experiment, hitchhiking with a friend along the East Coast in 2000, he complained in an email to friends, "We've been trying to live without money, but people slipping massive amounts of it into our pink little hands has raised questions of what we should do. I made a rule: I would get rid of it before sunset, either give it away or spend it, usually on some little treat I didn't need, like a chocolate bar. But then that sunset rule turned into sunrise." Finally he decided not to spend the money at all, but rather to give it away.

But a ride in a friend's car meant using gas that someone was going to have to pay to replace. "Maybe if we just wait here someone will give us gas," Suelo proposed on one occasion. "Or we'll find some." The friend opted to fuel up with his own money.

In the spring of 2001, Suelo had his one major lapse. While staying at a commune in Georgia, wondering how he was going to get back to Utah for a friend's wedding, a most tempting and confounding piece of mail arrived: a tax return in the amount of five hundred dollars.

"This experiment of having no money is on hold now," Suelo wrote in a mass email to friends and family. He cashed the check, paid the deposit on a drive-away car, and blasted across America at the wheel of a brand-new, midnight-blue, convertible Mercedes-Benz 600 sports coupe.

"What a kick it is to go from penniless hitchhiker to driving a Mercedes!" he wrote. "I got a deep breath of the southern US all the way to New Mexico, riding most the way with the top down and the wind making me look like a dust mop. On top of that, I get so much pleasure seeing the look on hitch-hikers' faces when a Mercedes stops for them. And dumpster-diving in a Mercedes is an absolute scream! Everybody should try it. It's almost as fun as hitching in the back of a pickup. Almost."

Later that summer he ditched the remainder of the money

"because it felt like a ball and chain," and has not returned to it since.

. . .

ON A SUNNY October afternoon, a few days after the watermelon feast, I follow Suelo up the canyon. He wears a plaid shirt and a ranger's olive-green trousers cut off at the knee—an attractive find in the discards of a national-park town, although a friend who made a similar score was cited for "impersonating a park ranger." Suelo's bolero hat completes the outfit. The flat brim and strap make me think of a Peruvian peasant, or a witch doctor. "I found this in the dumpster of the Christian thrift store," he says. "It was a child's cowboy hat. So I soaked it and stretched it and flattened it out. Fits perfect. Funny thing about that thrift store—they throw away all the good stuff and try to sell the crap. Anything that's old and made out of wool, if it has a tiny hole in it, they toss it. But they resell all the cotton T-shirts made in sweatshops."

Near the trailhead, he hides his bike in a thicket, scooping apples and potatoes from the crate into a threadbare backpack. Suelo has acquired and discarded many bicycles over the years. His current ride, which he has painted with Anasazi petroglyphs and decked with pink plastic flamingos, was a gift from his parents. He maintains it with parts and tools from a volunteer-run bike shop, and pulls used tires and tubes from the trash bins of retail stores. He doesn't own a lock.

As soon as we leave the asphalt he slips off his sandals, tucks them into the pack, and grips the desert floor barefoot. His feet are leathery and wide and cracked at the heels. He pads along the rocky trail.

The canyon is dizzying. Golden cliffs tower on both sides,

ravens circling on the updrafts. We walk beneath ancient petro-glyphs pecked into the rock—bighorn sheep and bigheaded humanoids. Along the base of the walls, the sandy bluffs are dotted with piñon pines and juniper and sagebrush, their trunks gnarled by the baking sun, roots burrowing into the sandstone cracks for a drop of moisture.

At first glance, the country appears uninhabitable. Above the canyon lies a badlands of stone fins and arches and dry gulches that has inspired place-names like Devil's Garden, Fiery Furnace, and Hell's Revenge—the kind of landscape in which Hollywood actors stumble upon a human skeleton picked clean by vultures, finger bones clutching a dry canteen. But at the bottom of the canyon, a cool green stream bubbles over the slickrock, carving porcelain bathtubs and plunging over algae-streaked falls into deep, clear swimming holes. Leafy willows and cottonwoods cling to the banks, dropping yellow leaves into the swirl. Beavers have chomped the soft trunks, building lodges and ponds that shimmer in the shady oasis. The air is sweet with the smell of Russian olive trees.

The trail turns to sand, and the grit pours into my shoes, so I follow Suelo's lead and remove them. At a shallow spot in the canyon, hundreds of small green shoots rise from the sand. "Wild onions," Suelo says, kneeling and digging away at the tendrils. I dig one, too. "Careful not to pull too hard," he says, "or it'll break." He rummages through his pack for a metal spoon, and digs with that. We each harvest an onion, stripping the fibrous husk from the bulb. "You can eat the whole thing," he says, curl-ing the green stalk around the white tuber and popping it in his mouth. I do the same. It's delicious—a sweet, tangy chive.

We drop into the shade and wade across the stream. A raven caws overhead and Suelo caws right back in perfect imitation.

After about an hour, we leave the trail and scramble up a shallow gulch. Suelo hops between rocks, avoiding the sand and grass. "I try not to leave footprints," he says.

In a shady alcove where black streaks of springwater stain the cliff, we climb a steep talus slope and arrive at his current cave, a spacious twenty-by-twenty cavern with a commanding view of the opposing cliffs and brilliant blue sky. Beside a fire ring, a deflated sleeping pad lies in the dirt, along with a sleeping bag, a few articles of clothing, a guitar, and Suelo's most recent score: an expensive pair of binoculars. "I found those in a dumpster," he says with evident delight. "So I decided to become a birder." So far he has glassed a great blue heron, a hawk, and a pygmy owl.

Suelo drops his pack and carries a scuffed plastic soda bottle down canyon to a rain pool, where he hops across a quicksand bog and crouches to fill the bottle. He harvests handfuls of wild grasses, pine needles, juniper sprigs, and mallow leaves.

"People are always giving me wheatgrass," he tells me. "And I thought, well, why not use wild grasses? So I've been drinking it most every morning. And I've been feeling really good."

He sits cross-legged on a foam pad in the dirt and lights his stove—a blackened number-ten chili can with the lid removed and a hole cut on the side. Into the opening he feeds twigs, until a fire burns inside the can. He sets a pot of water directly on top. Holes poked in the side of the can provide ventilation, and within just a few minutes the water is boiling. Suelo lowers his bundle of wild herbs into the pot and lets them steep.

Between the wilderness approach, the soot-covered cave, and the gray-haired wise man steeping herbs over a flame, a visit with Suelo starts to feel like some Himalayan trek to the guru. And it's true that conversations with him turn quickly to religion and philosophy. On this particular trip, Suelo is hosting what you might call an apprentice, a young man from Indiana who has been studying martial arts and Eastern religion for a decade, and after reading about Suelo on the Internet took the Greyhound west to learn moneyless living from the master.

Suelo quickly deflates any perception of himself as a holy man, however. The deeper he gets into philosophy, the more he laughs at himself, averting his eyes when he says something particularly insightful, as if embarrassed to reveal his deeper knowledge. He is chronically forgetful, rubbing his forehead and saying things like "I can't remember if I went to India before or after I went to Alaska." He has a disarming habit, when presented with some fact he already knows, of exclaiming, "Oh, yeah!" or "Ahh!" as if he were learning it afresh.

Me: "I read that the Buddha was born a Hindu."

Suelo: "Oh, yeah! You're right!"

What's more, Suelo's sense of humor is strictly goofball. Upon hearing that a tract of land beside the cemetery is to be developed into houses, he says, "I hear people are just dying to get into that neighborhood!"

While I ask him what he has learned from living without money, he beats back a column of smoke from the second round of tea. I note that he has taken on a certain Oz-like appearance, answering from behind the curtain of smoke. He waves his hands like a sorcerer and intones in a wizardly voice, "Now I have entered the mystical realm!" He busts up at his own joke. "I am a genie in a bottle!"

· · ·

WITH FOUND AND discarded objects, and a construction budget of zero, Suelo has turned his current cave into a postconsumer hobo paradise. When he first discovered it, the floor was rocky and uneven, so he hauled buckets of sand to level it. He piled boulders at the mouth to block wind and visibility. He collected discarded pots, pans, bowls, plates, knives, forks, spoons, and spatulas. In a sealed plastic bucket he stored rice, flour, noodles, oatmeal and grains, as well as root vegetables like potatoes and carrots, which can last for months in the dry, cool cave. Now fresh groceries hang from the ceiling in a cotton bag, safe from mice and ringtail cats.

Tucked beneath a north-facing cliff, the cave never gets sun, and even in the daytime it is chilly. As darkness falls, he lights his lamps. While Suelo sometimes finds functional flashlights, the batteries eventually die. Oil lamps arranged on small rock ledges around the cave are a more reliable light source. To make one he simply fills a glass jar with vegetable oil, then inserts a short length of cotton cord into a wine cork, which floats on top. A tinfoil barrier keeps the cork from catching fire, and the wick burns for days.

That night I unroll my bag across the fire ring from Suelo and, gazing out the cave and up at the bright silent stars, quickly fall asleep. When I awake just after dawn, Suelo is sitting cross-legged on his pad with his sleeping bag draped over his shoulders. He sits perfectly still facing the canyon as the sun creeps down the far walls. Then he lies back down and sleeps awhile longer.

After morning tea we move out of the cave onto the sunny rock ledges where Phil, the apprentice, leads a session of Qigong, a meditative Chinese martial art. We cycle through such postures as Embracing the Tree and Catching the Ball. With sunlight pouring over the rim and wrens singing, the moment swells toward unreasonable bliss, until Suelo swings at me with some honky karate chops and blurts in his best Bruce Lee accent: "Now we fight a match to the death!"

Although he lives with great intention, Suelo seems to go whichever way the wind blows. When he finds binoculars, he takes up birding. When he finds a guitar, he takes up music. When a martial artist arrives in his caves, he takes up Qigong. And so on. "Randomness is my guru," he told me.

As such, canyon life is idyllic. Once it warms up, he will take a dip in the creek. When he doesn't feel like going to town, he can survive for a week or more on his stores and what he forages. As we sit there in the sun he plays a melody on a wooden flute someone carved for him. Juniper and sage and the spindly reeds of Mormon tea shrubs rise out of the bench.

Yet Suelo does not become too attached. He knows that at any moment a ranger could arrive and whisk him along. The cave does not belong to him. His residence here is explicitly against the law.

"This is a nation that professes to be a Christian nation," he tells me, surveying his temporary kingdom. "And yet it's basically illegal to live according to the teachings of Jesus."

Expecting anybody to follow the teachings of Jesus—least of all the United States government—sounds like a pretty naive view of the world. Yet that's how Suelo was raised, in a family of religious idealists who, like him, don't accept that modern times are fundamentally different from the times of the prophets and heroes.

3

. . .

ONE DAY WHEN he was eleven years old, Daniel returned from playing in the yard to find the house empty. The year was 1972 and the family was living in the suburbs of Denver, where Daniel's father worked at a car dealership. Daniel called for his parents and siblings. No reply. His three older brothers were not in their room. His older sister was nowhere to be found. He called their names, his voice trembling. He rushed to his parents' bedroom. His mother's clothes lay atop her shoes. She would never leave clothing on the floor. It was as if she had vaporized while standing in them. "Mom!" he cried. "Dad!" An electric fan whirred.

Daniel's mind raced for some benign explanation. Maybe they'd taken a walk with the dogs. Or driven somewhere. But the car was in the driveway. Try as he might to interpret these clues in some other way, he fixated on what struck him as the only plausible scenario: Rapture. The Lord had returned and sat in final judgment. The righteous, including Daniel's family, had ascended to heaven. As for the sinners, they were doomed to suffer the tribulations prophesied in the Book of Revelation. Fires would rain down from the skies and wicked Babylon would plunge into the sea. As poor Daniel stared trembling at his mother's shoes, he could only conclude that while she and the rest of his family had soared up to heaven, he, in punishment for some unspeakable sins, had been *left behind*!

When the family clomped up the front steps—they'd been over at the neighbors' house—they found Daniel crying. They comforted him and had a gentle laugh. He was the youngest, and so worried about everything. He shouldn't fret so much. When the end-times did arrive, he would be going home to Jesus.

In a family of biblical literalists, Daniel was the most literal of them all. One summer when he was very young, he stockpiled his dollars and quarters and bought Christmas presents for Mom and Dad, for Pennie and Rick and Ron and Doug. He wrapped them with Santa Claus paper and presented them in the August heat. He wanted them to enjoy their gifts here on earth, before the Great Tribulation.

Daniel felt like he was the only kid in Sunday school who took it seriously. But that didn't make faith easier. The kids who goofed off and passed notes didn't lie awake fretting about Mathew 19:24, wondering how a full-grown camel could squeeze through the eye of a needle, and if so, why such an event was more likely than a rich man entering the Kingdom of Heaven.

For those not raised fundamentalist, the Rapture seems a cartoonish fairy tale. But in the past half century the notion has become mainstream. As the percentage of Americans belonging to mainline Protestant denominations has steadily dropped since the mid-1960s from a quarter to a tenth, those belonging to evangelical or fundamentalist churches have held fast at about 25 percent. Factoring in population growth, that firm percentage reflects an increase in numbers. In the popular imagination, the child's nightmare of burning in hell with the devil and his pitchfork has been replaced by the Apocalypse of the Book of Revelation, with its four horsemen and pits of boiling sulfur. Those raised in the faith accept as fact that this world's days are numbered. Clocks will stop, and time as we know it will cease.

Suelo's family typifies the nation's drift toward fundamentalism. They are part of the counterweight to the great secular shift that was also occurring over the past half century, making Americans—my family, for instance—less religious and more educated, urban, and prosperous. I had assumed that a conservative Christian family would be less accepting of a son who chose to be homeless. I was wrong. For fundamentalists, living in a cave and eating locusts and wild honey is a less far-fetched way of life than it seems to secular people concerned with getting a good internship and scoring high on the SAT. The guiding mythology of the Shellabarger family is not the American Dream, in which wealth waits as the reward for a lifetime of hard work. Theirs is a deep idealism in which faith trumps everything, and money never matters much. For all of his eventual rebelling, Suelo's upbringing actually *prepared* him for quitting money.

. . .

AT EIGHTY-TWO, Dick Shellabarger is still a lumbering fellow, with a sprawling six-foot-five frame and big hands and big feet. He fills the room like a Clydesdale. His booming voice carries a twang as he drops cowboyisms: *I says to him, no way* and *The Lord don't care about that.* "Money is the public God," he bel-

lowed as a way of welcoming me. "They do anything possible—
kill, murder, and lie—for it."

Dick has been married to Daniel's mother, Laurel, for more
than sixty years. They live in Fruita, Colorado, a farm town that
is being overtaken by the sprawl of Grand Junction, fifteen miles
to the east. They're about one hundred miles from their youngest son's cave. The cul-de-sacs named Comstock and Mother-
lode are empty except for children on bikes and mothers pushing
strollers. American-made cars and trucks fill the double driveways, with bumper stickers that say RESPECT LIFE. The Shellabarger home is a single level of brick and stucco and wood siding,
with a pair of evergreens on the lawn. On the front door hangs
an inscribed placard: *Therefore if any man be in Christ, he is a new
creature.* The house, which is owned by Dick's older brother, is
plain and clean: three bedrooms and two bathrooms, textured
walls all the same neutral shade of off-white. In the garage,
between meticulously organized hand tools and coiled extension
cords, is a nondescript sedan.

The youngest of five children, Dick Shellabarger was born in
1928, on the cusp of the Great Depression, and raised in Colorado.
His father, a mechanic and barber and jack-of-all-trades, hopped
freight trains to California in search of work. After working as a
truck driver on the construction of the Alaska-Canada Highway,
he parlayed his earnings into two cow ponies and a ranch near
Denver. Dick grew up on a horse, moving from one place to the
next as his dad sold one ranch and bought another. "I was trying
to go to high school in Castle Rock, taking two or three buses to
get there," Dick says. "I finally had to quit after tenth grade."

The family never got ahead, unable to obtain a loan for the
initial livestock. They did keep afloat a dude ranch that offered

horseback rides, and an old lodge with a bar, jukebox, and dance floor. Dick's older brothers left home and built an empire of car dealerships, but Dick took after his father, tinkering with one thing and another. After an army stint in Japan, he supplemented his summer income at the ranch by breaking the neighbors' horses.

If Suelo inherited his itinerant nature from his father, then his contemplative side comes from his mother. Laurel is a year older than her husband, a real beauty with regal carriage and sparkling eyes and fine cheekbones. Laurel Jeanne Wegener was born in Denver in 1927 to first-generation Americans whose parents had emigrated from Germany. Her father, Charles, was a traveling salesman and woodworker. The family struggled during the Depression, buying groceries on credit. But Charles—who like a European of the previous century played the flute, dressed in dark suits, and never learned to drive, preferring trains and trolleys well into the automobile era—insisted that his daughters learn classical piano and sing in a choir.

Although the family was nominally Christian, they were not devout. "I went clear through the catty-chism at the Lutheran church," Laurel says. As she matured into a striking and proud young woman, her commitment to the religion proved thin. One day she walked to church for a field trip, arriving just as the bus was pulling away. She ran after it, waving and hollering, but the bus didn't stop. "And guess who got mad," she says. Laurel never went back.

Perhaps it was her parents' European refinement, but Laurel was just plain dissatisfied with the life that wartime America offered. After graduating, she worked as an usherette in a movie theater, then earned a certificate in calculation from the community college and got an accounting job. After a few months she thought, *Good grief, is this all there is?*

The year was 1946, decades before fundamentalism reached the mainstream. "Born again" and "personal savior" were phrases cried out under revival tents, not under the dome of the United States Capitol. Billy Graham's evangelical crusades would not begin until 1948, and Jerry Falwell would not found his church until 1956. (Though some might quibble, I use the terms "fundamentalist" and "evangelical" interchangeably. Both describe a faith based more on a literal Bible reading than on membership in an organized church.) As the size and scope of secular government increased during the New Deal and World War II, and mainline churches focused on social justice instead of personal salvation, more Christians responded to what looked like the apocalypse—D-day, Auschwitz, Hiroshima—by seeking the moral certainty of scripture.

One night, listening to her parents' radio, Laurel tuned in to the warm voice of a preacher on *The Old Fashioned Revival Hour* broadcast from California. He spoke of missionaries in Africa, saving souls on the hot plains and deep in the jungle. Now, that sounded like a fulfilling—and exciting—life. Laurel enrolled at the Denver Bible Institute. On the first day, the teacher unrolled a sheet of paper and drew a time line outlining the seven eras of human existence, corresponding to the seven days of Creation. The Dispensation Chart. The First Dispensation was the Creation. The Second spanned the 1,656 years from Adam to Noah, the Third encompassed the next 430 years to Abraham, and the Fourth covered the following 1,960 years to Jesus. Ever since then, the teacher announced, we had been living in the Fifth Dispensation, or the Church Period, which would come to a catastrophic close with the return of Christ, and the advent of the Sixth Dispensation: the Great Tribulation. In this violent period lasting only seven years, the prophecies of the Book of Revelations would come to pass: the seven seals would be opened, Christ would sit in judgment, fires would burn down from heaven, Satan would boil in sulfur, and all of wicked humanity—Babylon—would be cast into the sea like a millstone. When the ash cleared, the true believers, the righteous Christians, would go forth into paradise and the Seventh Dispensation: the Millennium. Having destroyed Babylon, Christ would rule the New Jerusalem. The martyrs and saints would be resurrected, the Twelve Tribes of Israel restored, and the lion would lie down with the lamb.

"I was saved," Laurel says now. "I went home that night and asked Christ to be my personal savior." She spent the next three years in Bible college. The teacher took her under his wing like a daughter, and she traveled to Bible camps to testify. She preached the gospel to her parents, and they, too, were born again.

In the fall of 1948 she took a vacation. The bus dropped her seven miles from the guest ranch. Two cowboys leaned against an old Studebaker pickup. She locked eyes on the younger of them, a strip of rawhide in Levi's and boots and a Stetson, six foot five and 150 pounds. She squeezed between the two men in the cab of the pickup as it rattled toward the ranch. Every time the truck hit a bump, her knee banged against the skinny cowboy and a volt of something thrilling crept up her spine.

They arrived at the ranch and Laurel was led to her quarters, a sparse wood-planked cabin with a cot, smelling like pine needles and mothballs. Although the lodge was closed, Dick Shellabarger plugged in the jukebox. "I put some music on and we danced," he says today. "Just the two of us."

By the next day, they couldn't stay apart. Dick invited Laurel to have a look at a private cabin that he took care of. They walked together in the cold wind, closing the heavy wooden door behind them. He struck wooden matches and lit the kerosene lamps. He unfolded fresh bedsheets and together they spread them over the mattress. Then he knelt by the fireplace and wadded newspaper and stacked kindling and lit a match. Laurel discovered a piano and sat at the bench. Dick remembers the music she played as something ethereal, romantic, divine—nothing like the honky-tonk he was used to. He hovered behind her, swallowing her sweet scent and breathing the melody. His hands removed themselves from his hips, ventured forward unsteadily, and came to rest on her face.

Laurel leaped up from the bench in a tumble of chaotic notes. She turned, gave her suitor a peck on the cheek, and fled into the starry night. Dick ran after her. It was dinnertime, and he could smell his mother's fried chicken. He stumbled into the kitchen, lobbed his hat onto a hook, and took the last vacant seat. Everyone was there: Mother, Father, two brothers, a cousin— and Laurel. He shot her a nervous glance, then returned for an awkward stare. Something was wrong. The rosy flowers beneath those delicate cheekbones were black bruises. He gazed helplessly. There on her face for all to see was the evidence of his indiscretion—the prints of his sooty fingers.

· · ·

SIXTY YEARS LATER, the Shellabargers are still crazy for each other. Dick still talks like a ranch hand, and Laurel still corrects him.

"We used to call Dad the original railroad bum," he told me as I sat in their living room.

"But he wasn't a bum," Laurel said.

"No, he wasn't. We were just joking with him. I wish I had his skills."

"You do," said Laurel. She turned to me. "He just doesn't give himself credit."

"My grandfather was a barber," Dick told me.

"A cosmetologist," Laurel insisted.

That night, heading into the bedroom they had readied for me, I paused in the hallway outside their office and listened. Dick sat at his desk, dictating an upcoming Bible lesson while Laurel transcribed the notes so that a deaf girl in the class could read along as he lectured.

"Verse nineteen," he began, clearing his throat. "Capital *I*. I will betroth you to Me, capital *M,* in righteousness and in justice, comma, in loving kindness and in compassion, period."

I knew that they had computer programs and the Internet, from which they could cut and paste this verse. But they enjoyed the ritual, he the preacher, she the scribe. Dick Shellabarger continued: "Verse twenty. Capital *A.* And I will betroth you to Me, capital *M,* in faithfulness, period. Capital *T.* Then you will know the LORD, all capitals, period."

. . .

AMONG EVANGELICAL CHRISTIANS, all of whom await the Second Coming of Jesus, there are historically two camps: postmillennialists and premillennialists. For most of the seventeenth and eighteenth centuries, most were of the "post" variety, meaning that they expected the Messiah's return after the thousand-year reign of peace. In order to hasten His arrival, they set out to create that harmonious world here and now, fighting for the abolition of slavery, prohibition of alcohol, public education, and women's literacy.

The chaos of the Civil War and industrialization caused many evangelicals to rethink their optimism. They determined that Jesus would actually arrive *before* the final judgment. Therefore any efforts toward a just society here on earth were futile; what mattered was perfecting one's faith. As historian Randall Balmer writes, these believers "retreated into a theology of despair, one that essentially ceded the temporal world to Satan and his minions."

This schism widened in the twentieth century. After the 1925 Scopes Monkey Trial in which fundamentalists were humiliated by the national press, premillennialists retreated into their own subculture, shunning the politics and causes of the times. "They turned inward," writes Balmer, "tending to their own piety and seeking to lure others into a spiritualized kingdom in preparation for the imminent return of Jesus."

When Dick Shellabarger proposed to Laurel, just months after they met, she was planted firmly in the camp of the premillennialists, and said she could only marry a like-minded Christian.

"My parents have belonged to a church all our lives," Dick said.

"That's not enough."

"How could that not be enough?"

"Is it personal?" she asked him.

As it turned out, the theological distance Dick would have to travel was not very far. The church to which his family belonged, however loosely, was the Plymouth Brethren, a sect founded in Ireland in the 1820s by John Darby, the very author of the Dispensation Chart that had captivated Laurel. Dick's grandfather was a lay minister who had memorized the entire New Testament.

Dick was saved, and in 1949 the Shellabargers married and joined the Plymouth Brethren. The faction is so certain of the Bible's literal truth that Southern Baptists look loose by comparison. The Brethren hold that God ought not to be worshipped in a denominational church with a professional minister. They call their buildings "chapels" to reflect their belief that a church is a holy fellowship of believers, not the mere structure where they meet. They believe that orders like Catholics and Lutherans, by building such massive earthly organizations, have strayed from the teachings of the Bible. For fear they will be perceived as just another denomination, they usually don't use the name Plymouth Brethren officially, which is why most Americans have never heard of them.

For six decades, Dick and Laurel balanced their service to Christ with the material needs of raising a family. Because the Brethren had no paid pastors, Dick served as a lay minister. Women were not allowed to preach, but Laurel led Bible study groups. Nonetheless, as newlyweds they needed an income. Dick's parents had closed the guest ranch, and without a high school diploma, his options were limited. He landed a job on a Montana ranch, sight unseen. In 1949 he overhauled an old Buick and drove north with his bride and their few belongings. Upon arriving, they discovered that the wife of the rancher had fallen ill, and couldn't work.

"Your wife can do the cooking," said the rancher.

Instead of capitulating, Dick displayed a trait he would one day pass on to his son: the refusal to work under unfair conditions.

"I intend on her not working," said Dick. "She's pregnant."

"Well, that's the deal we had."

"No, it's not."

"That's what was in the letter."

"I just happen to have the letter in my pocket." Dick whipped out the paper and unfolded it.

"Well, she's going to cook and that's it," said the rancher.

Dick cocked his fists, and the rancher turned and ran. The Shellabargers repacked the Buick and headed home.

Dick took a job in a print factory, but when required to run off a batch of girlie calendars, he quit. The couple learned that they were just different from their coworkers. "They thought we were self-righteous goody-goody two-shoes," Dick says. "It's always been like that. When I traveled to conventions, I didn't drink, didn't go to the prostitutes. I had to push them off my lap." After the birth of their daughter, Pennie, Dick attended a Brethren college in Chicago. Their first son, Rick, was born. The young family lived in a cramped flat for three years while Dick learned the Word. "I was an old hillbilly pounding the streets south of Chicago, in the all-black ghetto," he says.

Dick worked a series of jobs in car dealerships and printing factories, uprooting the family every few years. He and Laurel had three more sons along the way. In the Colorado mining town of Gypsum, they started a Brethren meeting. ("We brought a beekeeper to Christ," Laurel remembers.) Laurel stayed home to raise the children. Neither parent pursued a permanent career: their true calling was the Lord.

Their last-born was Daniel James Shellabarger, delivered in 1961 in Arvada, a suburb of Denver. After Daniel's birth, Dick took a job at his brother's Chevy dealership. The next year he was hired by Denver Volkswagen, then in 1967 promoted and transferred to the national office in San Antonio, Texas, which is where Daniel began first grade. For a string of good years Dick jetted around the country to conventions and dealerships.

The family's idealism reigned. On holidays in San Antonio, the Shellabargers would pack all five kids into a VW Beetle—Doug and Dan stuffed in the "way-back" hatch—and drive to the Mexican border. The gates were flung open and Mexicans would flood in over the Rio Grande bridge to spend the day shopping and visiting relatives. Dick and Laurel and the kids greeted them on the side of the road, armed with fistfuls of evangelical tracts in Spanish. None of the family spoke the language, but that didn't matter. All seven would pass out the pamphlets and say *Hola* and *God Bless*. "Mexicans are just starving for the Word," Dick says. It wasn't quite a mission to Africa, but it was the life Laurel had always wanted.

While Daniel's Good News upbringing might seem anachronistic to many raised in the calamitous sixties and seventies, the Shellabarger family was the norm for many fundamentalists. "So comprehensive was this alternative universe," writes Randall Balmer, an evangelical himself by upbringing, "that it was possible in the middle decades of the twentieth century (as I can attest personally) to function with virtual autonomy from the larger culture and have, in fact, very little commerce with anyone outside." As with fundamentalists of all stripes, the Plymouth Brethren insist that theirs is the only true way among all other types of Christianity—to say nothing of other religions. This is why, in a 78 percent Christian-majority nation like America, many evangelicals consider themselves a besieged minority. "We believed growing up that everyone outside our church was evil," Suelo says now. "Not to be trusted."

Those years of relative wealth in San Antonio turned out to be the exception. After a series of mergers, Dick lost his job in 1969 and returned the family to Denver, where Daniel started middle school. He grew into a small, serious boy. While Ron and Doug had inherited their father's loping frame, Rick and Daniel had the fine bones of their mother. Daniel was anxious about being the smallest and the youngest; sometimes he wore a pair of boots with big blocky soles to try to be as tall as the others. He was often so nervous about going to school that he'd get sick and be allowed to stay home. Although he was sociable enough to make friends, the family's life of itinerant gospel-spreading took its toll.

"All the moving combined with my parents' idealism made it hard to have friends," Suelo says. "Especially when you're told that everyone outside of the family, or the church, is evil. People would tease us, but instead of fighting back we turned the other cheek. Now I realize that what kids want, when they tease, is to engage with you, to spar, and that's a way of making friends. But I couldn't see it then."

Although insular, the family was warm and well functioning. Childhood friend Randy Kinkel, who went to school with Daniel near Denver, recalls the Shellabarger home as laid-back and welcoming, graced by Laurel's radiant smile and filled with a menagerie of pets, including dogs, cats, birds, fish, even an alligator. "Dan fit in as much as a quiet, thoughtful kid can at that age," Kinkel says. "He was an incredibly funny kid, good at voices and mimicry, and also could draw very well. I don't remember thinking he was any kind of religious nut." Daniel and Randy's favorite lark was writing a fake newspaper in which the local kids' TV-show host, Blinky the Clown, was always drunk and causing trouble, explosions, death, and general mayhem. "The humor was very sophisticated for grade school," says Kinkel.

Daniel's preoccupations returned to religion. While his church preached that the Bible was absolute truth, sometimes its members didn't follow Jesus's teachings. Some of the Brethren, like Mr. and Mrs. Hatch, who donated the new Sunday school building for the plain stone campus in a working-class Denver neighborhood, arrived in Cadillacs, fur coats sleek in the winter sun. One Sunday in 1969, just as Mr. Hatch was opening the massive car door for his wife, an odd-looking character walked down the street: long hair, faded blue jeans, a Mexican blanket draped over his shoulder. A hippie, is what Daniel's father called the type. The hippie walked right up to Mr. and Mrs. Hatch and took in their Cadillac and furs with contempt.

"Is this what Jesus taught?" he said. "Are you serving God—or money?"

The Hatches were speechless. The hippie sauntered on past. Suelo stared after him, aghast, until his father tugged him into the chapel.

"Heathen," said his father. "He don't understand."

But Daniel couldn't shake the man's words. He had read the Gospels. Wasn't it true that Jesus had commanded us to cast aside our worldly belongings? Mathew 19:21: "If you want to be perfect, go, sell your possessions and give to the poor." And hadn't Paul written in Timothy 6:10 that the love of money was the root of all evil?

What if that heathen was right, and the Brethren were wrong?

· · ·

In 1974, in a fit of entrepreneurial zeal, Dick cashed in a life insurance policy and moved the family again, this time to tiny Safford, Arizona, to launch a Montgomery Ward catalog franchise. Just after Daniel celebrated his fourteenth birthday, the business failed. "He lost everything," Suelo says. In 1975, bankrupt and humbled, Dick brought his family to Grand Junction and once again accepted a warehouse job at a Chevrolet dealership owned by his brother.

There the family made the closest they'd come to a permanent home. The Shellabarger kids would attend high school and begin college there, and all but Daniel would marry. Grand Junction was a dusty oil and farm town, and a hub for rail and trucking, where the most exciting thing to do was ride the elevator to the top of the bank building. The largest city on the Western Slope of the Rockies, it lacked the charm of mining towns like Aspen and Telluride that would become luxury resorts. This was Nixon country, a stronghold of the silent majority, home to numerous churches and tough men with mustaches driving large pickup trucks. It suited Dick and Laurel fine. Like fundamentalists across the nation, they were emerging from decades of political apathy, and finding their voice in a new movement called the Religious Right. They were staunch conservatives who opposed abortion rights, homosexuality, and any intrusion by the government on their religious lives.

The family rented a clapboard cottage in a bleak neighborhood along the train tracks. Rick was living at home, and Ron, Doug, and Daniel were still in school, sensitive newcomers prone to getting picked on. Their one advantage was that with the name Shellabarger, they were assumed by the kids at Grand Junction High to be part of the rich family whose name dominated the billboards for the statewide Chevy dealers.

Around this time, Suelo began to question the sense of American exceptionalism that his parents had instilled in him. On a mission to Bolivia with a Christian group called Amigos de las Américas, in which North American teenagers gave vaccinations to South Americans, he developed some ideas about the nature of wealth, greed, and generosity that still influence him today. He traveled to the lowlands near the Brazilian border. It was Suelo's first glimpse of the Third World, at a time when Bolivia was second only to Haiti as the poorest nation in the Western hemisphere. "That was the first time I saw kids with bloated bellies," he remembers.

What impressed Suelo most was that despite their extreme poverty, the people were unfailingly generous. "They just had logs to sit on, and they'd get up and offer us seats," he says. "And they fed us. They barely had enough for their families but they made sure everywhere we went that we were fed. It just amazed me."

A few days after his return to Grand Junction, Daniel and a friend were walking through his neighborhood. By this time the Shellabargers had moved from the rental by the train tracks to a pleasant split level in the hills. As the boys approached a gaudy mansion on a corner, they cut across its lawn. A man raced to the door and yelled at them to stay off his grass.

It made Daniel think. The people who had the least were the most willing to share. He outlined a dictum that he would believe the rest of his life: the more people have, the less they give. Similarly, generous cultures produce less waste because excess is shared, whereas stingy nations fill their landfills with leftovers.

At about the same time, his belief in the infallibility of the church took its first blow. Upon moving to Grand Junction, Dick and Laurel had started a Plymouth Brethren home Bible study, and within a few years the group had raised enough money to build a chapel on the outskirts of town. But after only a few years, the Shellabargers had a falling-out with their congregation.

"We just plain didn't fit in," Dick says. "They started to find fault with us." The men in the church seemed to resent that Laurel held such a successful Bible study, even though she taught only other women. (Citing Scripture, Laurel believes it is wrong for women to teach religion to men.) "The women at Brethren were treated as inferior, as slaves," Dick explains. After three decades, the family left the Plymouth Brethren, and joined a nondenominational evangelical church.

By this time Dick had risen to manager at the dealership, and the family was again prosperous. Pennie had married an elder in the Plymouth Brethren and given birth to the first of what would be eight children. Rick and Doug had finished high school and were living at home and enrolled at Mesa State College in Grand Junction. After a year working in a hospital, Daniel joined them there. Ron, who suffered a mild mental disability, had married and was working as a laborer.

It wasn't until after he left home that Daniel's probing mind truly began to loosen the foundations of his faith. He decided he wanted to be a doctor, and he applied to transfer to the University of Colorado at Boulder. His family and church disapproved. They regarded Boulder as the Gomorrah of the Rockies, a haven for cults, liberals, and loose living. They thought the move would undermine his faith. But Daniel was firm. He thought any tests to his faith would only strengthen it.

4

. . .

To think, we must eat.

—Pierre Teilhard de Chardin

BEGGING MAY BE the most shameful act in America. It's how we define failure: if you don't work hard and get good grades, you'll end up on the street, panhandling for change. Traditionally the only more degrading means of supporting yourself is prostitution, although with the advent of legally sanctioned escort services, even call girls now command more respect than beggars.

In Eastern religions, begging has a whole different meaning. Hindu holy men called *sadhus* go door-to-door with a "begging bowl" that their neighbors fill with food. Ordained monks who live like sadhus are called *sannyasis*, from the Sanskrit word for "renunciation." For Buddhists it is the *bhikkus*, which translates as "beggars" or "ones who live by alms"; for Muslims the fakirs, which translates as "poverty"; for Sufis the dervishes, from the Persian word for "door," as in, the person who goes from door to door. In all these cases, the renunciates travel the countryside naked, or wrapped in a simple cloth. They often wear their hair in ropes and smear their bodies with clay and ash. They own nothing, earn no income, and survive entirely on the contributions of others.

Perhaps the most revered beggar of all time is Siddhartha Gautama. When he left his privileged Hindu home in 563 BC on the search for truth that would result in his becoming the Buddha, his only possessions were three robes, a razor, a needle, a belt, a water strainer, and a begging bowl. Giving alms was an act of exchange, not of charity. The purpose of begging was not to get food, but to humble oneself, to forgo one's own pride and admit to being dependent on others. In doing so, the renunciate offered the community the *privilege* of giving, so that they themselves could take a small step toward nonpossession, the quest upon which the holy man had embarked. The beggar received his bread, but the giver received something as valuable—the opportunity to share. The Buddha forbade his disciples from saying "thank you" as they collected alms. To this day some monks acknowledge the exchange by saying, "May your generosity bring you peace and harmony."

Far from being regarded as derelicts, *sannyasis* are afforded respect, as men who have renounced the material world for spiritual wisdom, which they share with the community that supports them. One notable adherent of *sannyasa* was Mohandas Gandhi, who declared, "I could not live both after the flesh and the spirit," as he chose poverty and forsook pleasures like sex and cooked food, even salt. Westerners have long viewed such asceticism with admiration, or at least curiosity. In *The Jungle Book* Rudyard Kipling sympathetically depicts a sixty-year-old Indian civil servant who, after raising his family and succeeding in his career, "had resigned position, palace, and power, and taken up the begging-bowl and ochre-coloured dresses of a Sunnyasi, or holy man." Even curmudgeonly Mark Twain, skeptical of American spiritualists like Brigham Young, was subdued into something like respect when he came across mystics in India in 1895. In *Following the Equator,* he wrote:

> *These pilgrims had come from all over India: some of them had been months on the way, plodding patiently along in the heat and dust, worn poor, hungry, but supported and sustained by an unwavering faith and belief. It is wonderful, that the power of faith like that can make multitude upon multitudes of the old and weak and the young and frail enter without hesitation or complaint upon such incredible journeys and endure the resultant miseries without repining. It is done in love or it is done in fear. I do not know which it is. No matter what the impulse is, the act born of it is beyond imagination, marvelous to our kind of people, the cold whites. There were "facquirs" in plenty with their hair caked with cow dung. There was a holy man who sat naked by the day and by the week on a cluster of iron spikes and did not seem to mind it. And another man stood all day holding his withered arms motionless aloft and was said to have been doing it for years. All these performers have a cloth on the ground beside them for receipt of contributions, and even the poorest of the poor give a trifle and hope that the sacrifice will be blessed to them. At last came a procession of naked holy people marching by and chanting, and I wrenched myself away . . . The memory of that sight will always stay with me, but not by request.*

There is simply no equivalent in modern Christianity, despite the fact that Jesus himself said, "Blessed are you who are poor, for yours is the kingdom of God. But woe to you who are rich, for you have already received your comfort." For centuries, renunciation was central to the religion. In fifth-century Syria, Saint Simeon the Stylite lived for thirty-seven years atop a tiny platform on a tower, fasting and making an endless series of genuflections. In the Middle Ages, European monks known as mendicants took up voluntary begging as a means of imitating Christ and expressing faith in divine providence. But the tradition did not last into the modern era, nor make the journey to the Americas.

To be sure, monks and nuns of the Franciscan and Carmelite orders still take a vow of poverty and are supported by donors. But these contributions are not collected on the streets. Nowadays alms can be given by credit card with a simple click at thefriars.org. Twentieth-century Catholics like Thomas Merton and Dorothy Day and her Catholic Workers strove to bring ascetic poverty into modernity. "We must frankly admit that self-denial and sacrifice are absolutely essential to a life of prayer," wrote Merton. But these renunciates populate only the fringe of Christianity. We can't imagine our monks or priests begging for food at our doorsteps; our charity for them stops at the Sunday collection plate.

While Suelo is not a monk and does not claim to belong to the ranks of holy men, he draws much of his inspiration from them. After a stint in a Buddhist monastery in Thailand, he briefly referred to himself as an American sadhu, and adopted a different take on begging. While his ethos prevents him from panhandling for money, he is willing to ask for food. Occasionally he goes to restaurants or bakeries and asks for leftovers. "Usually people are really nice. They are so glad they can give something. They smile. They go in the back and load up a plate. But sometimes I get, 'Fuck off. Get out of here.'"

"Is that humiliating?" I asked.

"Sometimes it is. That's part of the path, being able to walk away without reaction."

When I asked why he didn't wear a monk's robes and ask for alms, he said that he didn't think that religious people should receive more than anyone else. "The point is to lift everyone up in equality, to encourage people to help the bag lady or the drunk in the gutter as much as the Buddhist monk," he told me. "It might limit my ability to get food, but that's the concept of faith. It's all inward. If I'm following the path of truth, then I'm not going to worry about food, and I'm not going to manipulate people into giving me food."

The other reason he doesn't beg a lot is that his conservative Rocky Mountain upbringing instilled a certain pride in not asking for help. "That's been the hardest thing about this lifestyle," he said. "I was always raised to give. More blessed to give than to receive. For the first couple of years it was really hard for me to admit that I was in need. I still find myself doing that. Someone will ask me if I'm hungry, and I'm really hungry, and I'll say, 'No, I'm all right.'"

Of course our society has means of delivering food to the needy that don't require begging, primarily food stamps and nonprofit charities like soup kitchens. Suelo avoids them for the same reasons he shuns homeless shelters: the charity is not freely given. So without panhandling or the dole, how does he eat?

After our Qigong session as we sat outside the cave and watched the sun hover over the opposite cliffs, I pulled lunch from my pack. I had brought cheese and crackers and chocolate and an avocado. I watched Suelo closely. With all the talk about Jesus and ancient Hindus, I expected him to grind rice-grass seeds into flour with a mortar and pestle and then bake unleavened bread.

He revealed a clear plastic jar with an aquamarine lid that I recognized as the vessel for Skippy peanut butter. Instead of brown goop it was filled with brightly colored gemstones, red and yellow and orange and green. Crystals? He unscrewed the lid and extended the jar.

"Gummi bear?"

. . .

IN ALL MY visits with Suelo over the course of two years, he never appeared hungry or the slightest bit worried about where his next meal was coming from. Occasionally I cooked for him at my house or took him to a restaurant, but for the most part, he was the one feeding me. When I packed food up to his cave, so complete was his hospitality that I sometimes forgot to break out the grub. He had found his version of abundance.

To begin with, Suelo simply doesn't eat as much as most Americans. On a long walk, he might eat a hunk of bread and a couple of mandarin oranges, and decline the cheese and cookies I wolfed down. He typically eats just two meals a day, and they are simple: rice, fruit, vegetables, bread, cheese. He eats some meat, but not much. In this way his diet more closely resembles that of the typical human than the typical American. Americans eat 3,800 calories per day on average, while the world average is about 2,800. Suelo's diet puts him closer to a sub-Saharan African, who eats 2,200 calories a day.

Eating less has a long history in all religions. Moses, Jesus, Buddha, and Mohammed fasted regularly as a means toward purification and humility, as did modern spiritual leaders like Gandhi and Martin Luther King Jr. Catholics fast during Lent, Jews during Yom Kippur, Muslims during Ramadan. Mormons are encouraged to fast the first Sunday of every month. Buddhist monks typically eat breakfast around six, lunch at noon, then only liquids for the rest of the day. Although the practice has a variety of meanings, its general purpose is to focus less on physical needs and more on the spiritual realm. Suelo has incorporated this belief into his daily life. "Sometimes I get anxious that there won't be food today in the dumpster," he says. "But then I think it doesn't even matter if there's not. I could go for a couple of days fasting and I'd be fine. In fact it would be healthy."

Whatever food Suelo eats, he must procure. First, he forages. He digs for onions, nettles, watercress, wildflowers. He gathers pine and cedar needles to steep in boiling water for tea. He picks and dries mulberries from shade trees in town. He picks apples and peaches from abandoned orchards, rolling and drying them into fruit leather. Other parts of the country provide more bounty. He survived a month on the California coast on blackberries, kelp, fennel, sea pollen, and mussels. The mussels he threw onto a campfire until they cracked open like pistachios.

Over the years—both before and after quitting money—Suelo has tried his hand at harvesting live animals, with mixed results. He learned to spearfish in Alaska and lived for a few months on mostly salmon. But he has never been much of a hunter. He doesn't own a gun or a bow, and he doesn't trap. In the Arizona desert he chased wild javelina bare-handed without success. He does, however, occasionally find a dead mammal, usually roadkill. "I found this squirrel freshly killed on the river road," he wrote on his blog. "It had an acorn stuck between its teeth when I found it, plus about 14 acorns stuffing its cheeks!" He prepared the squirrel by skinning it, gutting it, and boiling it in a pot over a fire, more or less the method recommended in *The Joy of Cooking*. He fed it to his friends, and posted their photos of themselves nibbling the miniature carcass online. "Their looks of contentment say it all!"

Rodents notwithstanding, the Utah desert simply does not provide enough food for living off the land. In any case, Suelo would prefer to eat other people's excess than to harvest additional plants and animals. "I don't feel good about going in the canyon and hunting when there's enough food in the dumpster," he says.

Suelo's primary source of food, then, is what others have thrown away. Americans send 29 million tons of edibles to the landfill each year—that's 40 percent of our food. Much of it is over-the-hill produce: brown bananas, moldy berries, bruised apples, and wilted lettuce. But even more is perfectly good food, some still wrapped in plastic, that has merely reached an expiration date. Suelo gathers boxes of cookies, cans of corn, and packages of bacon that hours earlier would have sold at full price. He finds nonperishables like rice and flour and beans. In addition to the dumpsters beside grocery stores, those behind restaurants are often a good bet. Bakeries discard whole loaves at day's end, and pizza parlors chuck a lot of pies.

One day I set out with Suelo to gather food. Unlike begging, which in America is largely seen as degrading and pathetic, forcing the beggar to reveal his vulnerability to others, dumpster diving is slightly subversive, almost like stealing, a means of surviving by your wits. But success is not as simple as it sounds. Some fast-food chains instruct their employees to soil all throwaways with dishwater to discourage scavengers. And then there's the question of trespassing. To whom does the garbage belong? The property owner? The collection contractor? Or the public? A bin in an alley allows room for legal interpretation, but many markets keep their trash under lock and key, or sealed away in a loading bay. The supermarket dumpster we are raiding is inside such a cavernous room; clearly it sits on private property. But Suelo knows from experience that the rolling doors are kept open during business hours. "Just walk in there confidently," he advises. "Like you have a purpose. Nobody will bat an eye."

The next thing to know about dumpsters is that, unless they're full, they're hard to access. This one is five feet tall, five feet deep, and eight feet wide. We hoist ourselves up and rest our hips on the lip, then lower face-first toward the food, maintaining precarious balance by kicking our legs in the air. It's a vulnerable position; a gentle nudge behind our knees from a passerby would topple us into the container. What's more, after sixty seconds of dangling face-first into the heap, the blood is pounding in my ears and temples. We dig through the heap of refuse, heaving vegetables and bread loaves over our shoulder. The smell is sour and treacly. When finished, I pump my legs and push up from a bag of trash until I am upright, then slide back to earth. Some divers choose to climb into the dumpster. Then they can work in stealth and uprightness. However, being inside a trash bin creates its own set of anxieties. No longer are you merely picking trash; now you're in it. Escape is more difficult. And claustrophobic types fear that someone will walk by and shut the lid.

The bounty is as varied as it is rich. Here's what Suelo and I harvested that day:

6 loaves Pepperidge Farm bread
2 bags bagels
1 bag white potatoes
4 russet potatoes

1 box organic strawberries
2 packages raspberries
2 packages blackberries
1 grapefruit
7 packages sliced mushrooms
1 onion
1 squash
27 ears of corn

The quality of a dumpster's loot often reflects the neighborhood. Suelo's best scavenging was in tony Mill Valley, California, where he and a friend struck gold in the bins behind organic bistros and gourmet boutiques, feasting on lemon-drizzled hummus and roasted pepper panini. "We were eating high on the hog," he says. "There's so much good food in Marin County."

Much of what Suelo eats is simply given to him. Plenty of people invite him to dinner, or ask him to house-sit and help himself to whatever's in the fridge. He arrives at potlucks with whole loaves of bread and decent-looking fruits and vegetables. When he first quit money, he would often volunteer to work without asking for food in return. But after a couple of episodes in which he wound up dizzy and weak-kneed, he began asking for food in exchange for labor. It's the closest he comes to actual barter.

And then there are organizations that happily feed Suelo. A nonprofit farm called the Youth Garden Project in Moab holds a monthly "Weed and Feed" where volunteers spend a few hours pulling thistle and bindweed, and then are served a dinner largely from crops grown on the premises. Suelo swings a hoe at Sol Food Farms, a private farm with no paid employees, where a handful of volunteers are reviving an abandoned orchard and fallow fields with tomatoes and greens and cucumbers. In exchange for their labor, they take a portion of the harvest. I wondered if this wasn't barter—something Suelo refuses, as it violates the principle of giving without expectation of return. I asked the farm's owner, Chris Conrad, how he compensated Suelo.

"I tell him to take as much as he wants," Conrad said with a shrug. "But I don't even know if he takes it, to be honest. I don't keep track of that kind of thing."

The most reliable source of Suelo's nutrition in recent years was a volunteer-run free meal program that served lunch in a Moab city park 365 days a year. Each day, a rotating crew picked up leftovers from restaurants and school cafeterias, then served a hot meal to whoever came. Over the course of three years, without any government or church sponsorship—without even a permit from the health department—Free Meal served thousands of lunches. Suelo went nearly every day, occasionally staying afterward to wash dishes. It was a pretty festive event: a combination of the grizzled homeless men you'd find at a shelter, along with transient young rock climbers and backpackers, and office workers who stopped by on their lunch break—people who would never visit a food bank. The group's mission was not merely to feed the hungry, but also to prevent food from being hauled to the landfill, and in the process take the stigma out of eating free food.

"Free Meal is not classist or hand-down like your classic soup kitchen or welfare program," Suelo has written. "It is hand-across. Folks from all classes and needs and no-needs show up and sit down together for food that would otherwise be thrown out."

While Suelo appreciated the free food, what really brought him back was the community. "We crave community and friendship, but we want to have our own stuff," he says. "We don't want to be that way but we're addicted to our own isolation. A lot of it has to do with shyness in our culture. You have to overcome that. When I think about Latin America, there is a communal land tradition. The community goes out and harvests, and everyone works and celebrates and has fun. You can see people crave it here."

.   .   .

AT DUSK ON a cold night, Suelo and Phil, the apprentice and Qigong instructor, strike out in search of bananas. Suelo wears a black hoodie and backpack, with his hat hanging from his neck. A friend who lives on the other side of Moab has captured seventy pounds of bananas from a dumpster and sent word: get them while they last.

The twilight is clear and moonless, the rimrock black against the last pink in the sky. We pass several trash bins that Suelo assesses. "That one usually just has boxes and office papers. I might check it once a month." A source of perpetual griping among town scavengers is that the largest supermarket keeps refuse under lock and key. There is a single bin in the parking lot, however, where customers occasionally dispose of valuable items. "That's where I found my Therm-a-Rest, and those binoculars," Suelo says.

Although Moab is a small town, its sprawling layout is suited to drivers, not pedestrians. We cross the vacant grounds of the high school toward the ribbons of neon along the highway. Suelo and Phil tread silently the empty sidewalk between motels and car dealerships and fast-food outlets. 3.9% FOR 60 MONTHS OAC. MOAB'S BEST DEAL. KITCHENETTES-HBO-GUEST LAUNDRY. 10 LBS BAG OF ICE 99¢. Eighteen-wheelers rumble past, toward the Navajo Nation.

Approaching Pete's house, we pass a grocery store just closed. We creep down the alley to the loading docks, where electric light pools on the asphalt. Big machinery whines. I smell the acrid slicks of something sticky seeping across the lot. Suelo and Phil flip open the lids and peer in. The bins are piled high with black garbage bags that they peel open. Suelo pulls out a flat white paper box and sets it on the lid of the adjacent dumpster. The red-and-white flank of a Coca-Cola truck flickers in the dim light.

"Pizza, anyone?"

He retrieves another cheese pizza. He works efficiently in the darkness. He fishes out tubs of ranch dip and a pair of prepared meals in plastic platters from the deli and squints to read the label. "Some kind of spaghetti," he says. Then, surveying the growing mountain of food, he says, "Is there some sort of box we could put this stuff in?" A sack of bagels. Eight pieces of fried chicken sealed in a plastic sack.

Within five minutes, the men fill two large cardboard cartons, which they cradle as they depart the premises. Next door is a self-storage complex—often a good source for usable items, but tonight we find only windshields. We continue down a residential street.

"Pete's house is the kind where you don't have to knock," Suelo says. Inside the carport beside the recycling bins rises a mountain of food. A network of dumpster divers leaves their excess booty here, a warehouse for their friends to pick over. "A dump-store," says Daniel, with pleasure. Suelo is all but blind to the various leafy vegetables, cartons of muffins, and whole angel food cakes. He's come for the bananas. He peels one and munches, and then reaches for another.

Inside the house, a gray-haired woman washes dishes and a fluffy dog greets us. A food dehydrator whirs on the table and the place reeks of bananas. Moments later, Pete himself arrives, wearing a bike helmet. He has just returned from a ride around the neighborhood on his unicycle. We step back outside and stand around the food. The forecast calls for frost, and we wonder if the bananas will blacken. Daniel stuffs a bunch of bananas and the fried chicken into his backpack. Then he peels one more banana from the box and takes a bite.

"My brother used to call me Bananiel," he says.

We walk an hour in the dark cold night until we reach the trailhead. From the thicket where Suelo stores his bike, we retrieve three cans of beer. "Somebody—some unknown person—left them in my bike basket," says Suelo. And from there we pick our way up canyon in the black night.

It is an exaggeration to say that I cannot see my own hand in front of my face. However, I cannot see thorned branches at arm's length, and after a few whaps in the face, I hold my fist out like a boxer to protect my head. I set down my feet gingerly, not knowing if they will fall on rock, dirt, shrub, or water. Suelo strides quickly over the rugged terrain. We remove our shoes and cross the creek three times.

The next three crossings are narrow. "You can either take off your shoes," says Suelo, "or do the leap of faith." With that he carefully inches his way toward the bank, then jumps into the darkness, landing safely on the other side. This method works for me until the final crossing, when I misjudge the terrain and step to my shin in the chilly stream. We put on our shoes and Suelo leads us through a tangle of reeds and brambles in blackness. It occurs to me that over the years he has made this same dark trip hundreds of times.

We arrive at the cave at eleven-thirty, two and a half hours after leaving the banana stash. The temperature has dropped into the thirties, but I am warm from the walk. We are hungry. Daniel eats a banana, lights the oil lamps, and breaks out the bag of chicken. It's cold but good, greasy and salty and crunchy like deli fried chicken is. We three sit on the rocks devouring the breasts and thighs. Phil pops open a can of beer.

"I just got a bite that tasted like mold," Suelo says, holding the bag to the lamp and taking off his glasses to read. "It says it was packaged on the twenty-sixth."

We consider this revelation. It turns out that learning a chicken's date of preparation is not useful when nobody knows today's date. One thing is certain: none of us wants to stop eating. I, for one, haven't tasted any mold.

"Today couldn't be later than the twenty-seventh," Phil says.

"Yeah," Suelo says, lying back on his bed, propped against a slab of stone. He kicks off his boots and reaches for a second piece of chicken. "I'm sure it's fine."

. . .

ONE EVENING IN 2006, watching the sunset from the rock benches in front of his cave, Suelo decided to eat a cactus. He had been eating prickly pear for years, and he didn't see why a little barrel cactus would be any different. Besides, he had never heard of any cactus being poisonous. Not in North America, anyway. It went against evolutionary logic. The cactus's needles already protected it from predators: why, biologically, would it need toxins?

Suelo bent down and unearthed the cactus with a pocketknife. He skinned it, careful to shear all the needles, and slurped the whole thing like a kiwi fruit, just like he used to do when hopping trains across the desert, to stay hydrated.

Night was falling. Suelo basked in the warm evening air.

Then his heart started pounding. Faster and faster. His skin got hot. He felt like he was being lowered into a vat of boiling water. The burn spread up his calves to his thighs, over his hips and belly, rising up his neck until his entire head was on fire. His heart thumped. It couldn't take this.

I'm going to have a heart attack, Suelo thought.

The nearest hospital was a two-hour walk. He could hardly sit up. He crawled into his cave and lay there.

It wasn't like he was some clueless rookie out here in the wilderness. He had survived in these canyons for a decade. He couldn't believe this was happening. He had always talked, in the abstract, about how when it was time for him to go, he'd just lie down and die like a coyote, and surrender his earthly body back to the food chain. But he really didn't want to die just yet. And although he was not a sentimental man, he thought about his parents, a hundred miles away in Colorado. They loved him despite all he'd rejected of their beliefs. Already they'd lost one son, Rick, taken by a brain tumor at age forty-one. It was for their sake as much as anyone's that he scribbled his good-bye, which in his memory went something like this:

Well, life has been good, rich and full. I died happy. Don't worry about me. We all die. I ate some poison cactus. I love everybody.

How long would it take someone to find his body? He had plenty of friends in town, but they never came looking for him. Daniel arrived in town when he arrived, he left when he left.

Nobody really knew where he was. When would someone start to miss him? And who would find him first? Probably the ravens, and then the coyotes. Or maybe the ringtail. The ringtails loved to eat meat.

So really there was some justice. Ever since he'd given up money, certain people had called him a freeloader, a parasite. (As one comment-thread malapropist put it: "Do you Believe you are smooching off others?") They demanded to know what he was giving back. To which Suelo asked, Who says you need to give something back? What does a raven give? What does a barnacle give, or a coyote? In his view, every living thing gave plenty, merely by existing. But from a strictly materialistic view, his critics had an excellent point. A raven contributes nothing, except of course his own corpse, which will feed some other being. Now Suelo was dying, and he offered his body to the ravens, the coyotes, the ringtails, the mice, the ants.

Through the night he writhed and spat and prepared for death. Hours slipped away, but he was not aware of their passing. He knew only that he hadn't died—yet. And then, as the canyon rim appeared in silhouette against the gray sky of morning, he felt a swelling in his gut. Suelo hadn't vomited in twenty years, since battling dysentery in Ecuador, where he'd trained himself to plug all his orifices during all-day bus rides on bumpy mountain roads. But now he groped his way out of the cave, and there on the cobble below, heaved a torrent of green sludge. The beast was exorcised.

Tears in his eyes, Suelo began to grin, then laugh. The burning in his body was washed away by a cool wave of bliss. He wasn't going to die after all. He was alive!

. . .

SUELO LAUGHS AGAIN when he tells the story of his near death by cactus. But it raises the question of his health, especially as he ages; Suelo recently turned fifty. Medical care is expensive and difficult to obtain even for those of us with money. Food and shelter come easy by comparison.

"He's in a dangerous position," his father says. "In old age we won't be here. Things get tougher. He don't have any means of support."

Like a quarter of all Americans, Suelo lacks health insurance. He does not get Medicare. He does not have a regular doctor or dentist. Nonetheless, he is by all appearances in excellent health—far better than most people his age. He's lean and muscular, without a ripple of fat. He hadn't been sick in years when I met up with him. He can walk fifteen miles a day without fatigue. Basic tasks like packing food into the canyon or hauling buckets of water from the creek require and build muscle tone.

That said, Suelo doesn't perform anything that looks like exercise. He does not belong to a gym. He doesn't jog. Despite living in the outdoor sports capital of the world, he doesn't mountain bike or rock climb or kayak or ski. After meeting Melony Gilles, the watermelon eater, Suelo began attending her free yoga classes. (He arrived in rolled-up jeans and a dress shirt, but removed his hat for the postures.)

One reason for his good health is his fairly nutritious diet. Before quitting money, he had experimented with vegetarian and vegan and raw and organic diets, but these days he eats pretty much what he can get. Although the fried chicken and gummi bears are junk, he also eats plenty of rice and grains and fruit and vegetables. Being a scavenger doesn't exempt him from the basic dietary issues of our times: Suelo is convinced that he has a mild allergy to wheat and dairy, and after feasting on donuts or pizza, he complains of feeling drowsy and unfocused.

Suelo takes no pharmaceutical or recreational drugs and drinks very little alcohol. Instead he employs a number of home remedies to keep healthy. His friend Dr. Michael Friedman, a naturopathic M.D., thinks Suelo has probably contracted giardia, a water-borne parasite, from drinking out of wild streams— a common affliction in North America that causes diarrhea and stomach pain. Suelo follows the naturopathic principle of using the most natural, least invasive, and least toxic treatments available. He has found that swallowing a small portion of pine sap is a good cure for gastrointestinal distress.

One time while Dr. Friedman was camping with him in the canyon, they began discussing the medicinal properties of bee venom, said to contain an anti-inflammatory one hundred times more powerful than hydrocortisone. Some believe that it relieves arthritis, as well as the symptoms of multiple sclerosis. Suelo had been suffering joint pain of late. He and the doctor pondered the best way to experiment. Finally they decided to keep it simple. The two men marched up to a nearby hive and let the bees sting them. "It feels better already," Suelo reported, admiring his welts. He reported moderate pain relief, but did not repeat the treatment.

To the subject of eyeglasses, Suelo has devoted a few pixels in the Frequently Asked Questions section of his website:

My old eyeglasses broke several times, and I rebuilt them several times with melted plastic until they looked pretty goofy. Then they finally disintegrated a couple years ago. I was kind of happy about it and decided I didn't need eyeglasses. It would be like I was in a Monet painting, I thought. It was, and I was okay with it for about a year. But I started feeling embarrassed because I couldn't recognize my own friends at a distance, and they were thinking I was "stuck up." I decided I wanted to see more clearly again, and I was mentioning it to a friend. Another friend, Holly, who worked at the local thrift store, overheard our conversation and told me they had droves of old eyeglasses people donated, and to go and see if any fit my prescription and I could keep them for free. So I tried on several pairs, and the one that I thought looked most cool (Buddy Holly glasses) happened to be just my prescription. I've been wearing them since.

But the bane of Suelo's moneyless existence is dentistry. "I have gotten a couple cavities the past decade because I've eaten too many sweets," he writes. "Okay, I must be honest and say that teeth and mosquitoes are two things that get me to question the perfection of nature."

The remedy? Pine pitch—the same wonder sap from piñons that eases his intestines. Suelo claims that it is both a protectant and antiseptic, and he swears by packing the stuff directly into his teeth. "The summer I worked on the fishing boat I slacked in packing my first cavity in a molar and it grew until the pain was excruciating for about a day. I found my pinyon pitch and packed it again, and the pain vanished. But by that time the cavity was pretty deep, and half my tooth eventually broke off (without pain). I still have half a molar. Another tooth recently developed a cavity, which I've also been packing with pitch. It hasn't been hurting me."

I eventually learned that the poor condition of Suelo's teeth was not, as I had assumed, the result of living without money. Neither for that matter were they actually rotting. In fact he broke his two front teeth in a go-cart accident that occurred while he still had a job and a home. The reason he was unable to repair them was that, like many of us, he lacked dental insurance. In 2010, after years of suffering, Suelo got his teeth fixed. A friend of his parents, a member of their church who had traveled to the Third World to volunteer his services, offered to give Suelo fillings. "I'm not opposed to medical services if a doctor was willing to provide them voluntarily," Suelo says. "Then I would take them. I don't like a lot of organized do-goodism. The idea is take what's voluntarily given—and the people giving it aren't doing it because they're getting paid."

There was one time when Suelo did, in fact, accept medical help that was not given freely. Visiting his brother Doug in 2004 and helping build shelves, he gashed his thumb to the bone on a shattered jar of screws. Suelo was fairly certain that he could give himself sutures, but his sister-in-law insisted on taking him to the emergency room. The doc cleaned the wound and stitched it up, and sent Daniel on his way. The bill: a thousand bucks.

Suelo was not willing to just ignore the charge—at the root of his forsaking money is the desire to avoid debt. So he went back to the women's shelter in Moab where he volunteered, and asked if they would tally his hours, as if he were an employee, and cut a check directly to the hospital. After he had worked off about four hundred dollars of the bill, Suelo wrote to the hospital, asking if they thought it was ethical to charge one thousand dollars for seven stitches. The bills stopped coming.

.   .   .

IT'S ONE THING to forsake material goods like food and a home, or privileges like driving a car or flying on an airplane, but I wondered how far Suelo would take it. Would he get sick and die rather than compromise?

In the time I spent with him, Suelo caught a nasty flu that put him out of commission for a few days, but recovered without any medicine. Yet he is visibly aging. One night as we played a board game, he held the parts to within inches of his nearsighted eyes, complained that he was drowsy and "out of it," and finally excused himself to pedal back to camp and go to sleep early. As he gets older, if a mountain lion doesn't get him first, he'll begin to suffer the frailties of old age.

Sitting across the table from him in a conference room in the Moab library that we'd claimed as our own, I asked Suelo if he would rather die than get a five-dollar vaccination, or pay for a hundred-dollar hospital visit that could save his life.

"Yeah, I guess I'd be willing to die," he said. "If I broke my leg out in the wilderness, I feel it's natural selection. We all gotta die sooner or later anyway. And what makes one way of death worse than another? Is it really worse to die from a broken leg in a canyon than dying a few years later with tubes in my arm in a hospital, or extending my life—"

I interrupted. "If you fall off a cliff in the canyons and the ravens get you, that's kind of a romantic ideal. But what if you break your leg and don't die, and are hobbling around on crutches, and then you get gangrene? There are other ways to die that are pretty easily cured with modern technology. It's not like the only two ways to die are five years in a hospital bed or the instant death of falling off a cliff and breaking your neck."

Suelo was quiet a while, thinking about this.

"I guess that's where what people might call the superstitious, the religious part, comes in," he said. "If we're following our path, then *worrying* about what could or should happen is a worse illness than what could or should happen. And it's more likely we're going to be out of balance if we worry. The idea is that the future will take care of itself if we remain in the present. I really don't know what I'll do and I don't think about it that much. Some might call that irresponsible. But that's part of the path I'm on."

5

. . .

IN THE FALL of 1981, the first year of Ronald Reagan's presidency, Daniel Shellabarger neatly epitomized the conservative backlash sweeping the nation. He was clean-shaven and close-shorn. He wore white T-shirts and collared polos and crisp Levi's hiked to his belly button. Upon arriving at the University of Colorado at Boulder, he made a beeline for the fundamentalist Campus Crusade for Christ. In his first trip to the polls, he voted for Reagan. He had read a book by Soviet premier Brezhnev, and had learned that Communist agents were actively infiltrating every public institution in America, from its universities to the halls of Congress. He wrote an opinion piece for the campus paper on the subject. Watch your back, he warned. They're everywhere.

But for a young fundamentalist wading into scientific and ascetic currents, there was no better place to plunge into mysticism than Boulder, Colorado. The city was a vortex for wayfarers, the convergence of hundreds of alternative paths, from the Rocky Mountain Spiritual Emergence Network to the Jack Kerouac School of Disembodied Poetics at the Tibetan Buddhist Naropa Institute, on down the line to every manner of past-life regression, crystal healing, chart reading, psychic reprogramming, energy alignment, and planetary ascension. In a place the *New York Times* called the "New Age's Athens," a quarter of the residents had "undergone some type of New Age training." So pervasive was the anything-goes vibe that when in 1978 an egg-shaped spacecraft from the planet Ork landed on the college football field, the only thing the visiting alien had to do to assimilate was don a wacky pair of rainbow suspenders. In addition to launching the career of Robin Williams and adding "shazbot" to the lexicon, ABC's hit show *Mork & Mindy* introduced Boulder to the rest of the nation as a singularly far-out kind of town.

Orkan-like as Suelo was in this landscape, the place exerted a gravitational pull on him even as he parroted the beliefs of his parents. The Boulder campus, with its ivy-covered brick buildings and shaded lawns, was the quintessential academy, a place to discover life's truths. Soon he had made a circle of friends that included liberals, dreamers, agnostics, and drinkers. Daniel and his roommate—a lapsed Christian—stayed up late with them debating the existence of God, the meaning of love, the purpose of life. The conservatives at Campus Crusade seemed staid and incurious by comparison. He switched to Intervarsity Christian Fellowship, a collection of mainline denominations that was more progressive. "I didn't realize people could be Democrats and Christians at the same time," he says. Meanwhile he dropped his ambition of medical school and immersed himself in world religion, reading holy Scriptures of the faiths he'd been taught were pagan: Hinduism, Islam, Buddhism, Taoism. He made it his mission to visit a different church each week: Catholic, Pentecostal, Unitarian, Baptist, even a synagogue.

He continued to study the Bible, researching and beginning to articulate an interpretation that would consume his imagination in the short term and alter his beliefs thereafter. Daniel had always considered Christianity a male-dominated religion, with both the Lord and the Messiah taking male form. But as he studied the Old Testament's Book of Proverbs—King Solomon's exhortation to his people to embrace wisdom—he puzzled over the fact that wisdom was not merely an abstract concept. Wisdom was personified—as a woman: "Wisdom calls aloud in the street, she raises her voice in the public squares." Daniel traced this conundrum backward and forward in both testaments, examining all references to women, from Ruth to Mother Mary to Mary Magdalene, to Babylon the Whore, to the New Jerusalem, Jesus's millennial bride in the Book of Revelation. Proverbs 30 had always perplexed him:

> *There are three things that are too amazing for me,*
> *four that I do not understand:*
> *the way of an eagle in the sky,*
> *the way of a snake on a rock,*
> *the way of a ship on the high seas,*
> *and the way of a man with a maiden.*

And suddenly it hit him: You're not supposed to focus on the dominant—the eagle, the snake, the ship, the man. Rather, consider the recessive: the sky, the rock, the seas, the maiden. This is where the truth lies—in the feminine. He had stumbled upon something borderline heretical: the feminine side of God, a version of Christianity that resembled the archetypal Taoist observation:

Thirty spokes share the wheel's hub;
It is the center hole that makes it useful.
Shape clay into a vessel;
It is the space within that makes it useful.

"The Tao Te Ching says that it's the recessive that has the power," Suelo says. "And if you make it not recessive, it takes its power away. It's like roots. When they're underground they have their power. When you expose them to the light, they die. I started thinking about this idea: why do cultures veil the feminine?"

Home for the summer, Daniel presented his theory to his parents, proposing that the third part of the trinity—the Holy Spirit—was female. They found it compelling; after all, one of the reasons they'd left the Plymouth Brethren was its treatment of women, who were literally veiled—required to wear a head scarf during worship. They invited him to share it with their Bible study. But the rest of the congregation wasn't sure what to make of this wide-eyed college kid raving about *hokmah*, the Hebrew word for "wisdom." "Most of the time I'd just get silence," he remembers. "Polite silence. I could point it out in the Scripture right in front of people, and they could see there was something here we were missing. But then when I brought up this stuff that was against our Bible-reading tradition, now what do we do?"

Suelo pulled aside the pastor in the crowded foyer after the morning worship, and chewed his ear about Taoism and the recessive. The pastor shushed him and drew him close. "I don't share this with many people," he said, "but I do believe that the Holy Spirit is the feminine side of God."

Encouraged and feverish, Daniel dropped out of college and remained with his parents. He began writing a book: *Hokmah: The Feminine Side of God*. He bought an electric typewriter and clattered away. He returned to his hospital job, landing a night shift as a phlebotomist. Like the hero of some Dostoyevsky novel, Suelo shuttled between his vampire job drawing blood in the middle of the night and his parents' garret, where he toiled away at the manifesto that he was sure would rock Christendom to its foundation. One hundred pages. Two hundred pages. He rarely saw the sun. He slept in irregular intervals. The Truth was at hand, and he was on the verge of revealing it.

By the time Daniel returned to Boulder the next semester, he had finished a draft. He enrolled in a religious studies class with a professor named Brian Mahan, who was popular with spiritual seekers. Mahan was young and single and considered cool by students, one of the few profs so enthusiastic about the material that he'd continue discussions over coffee at the student union or a pie at Pizza Hut. A Catholic with degrees from the Harvard Divinity School and the University of Chicago, Mahan was smitten with liberation theology, the doctrine of social justice popularized in Latin America but condemned by the pope. Mahan's course was a meditation on the conflict between egoism and altruism, and he assigned an eclectic reading list that included William James, Sigmund Freud, Ayn Rand, and Martin Luther King. He didn't so much lecture as pose a never-ending series of questions, prodding his students to plumb their own intellects for answers.

Daniel left each class reeling with exhaustion, the ceiling of religious limitations lifting as the joists beneath his fundamentalism cracked. Emboldened by Mahan's amiability, Daniel met him privately and outlined his work in progress. Thirty years later, Mahan still remembers it.

"He was doing this huge project on exegesis, reforming the New Testament," Mahan says. "Very intelligent, very passionate, very sincere. I was impressed with the intensity and the intelligence. In those days in Boulder, you had some kids from the East Coast with a couple of bucks. You weren't used to kids working with this kind of single-minded intensity."

Damian Nash, a Christian raised in Boulder, was, like Daniel, also feeling his parochial beliefs explode. The two became best friends, and have remained so ever since. "Both of us spent teenage years as on-fire evangelicals," Damian says. "But intellectually we could no longer consider ourselves fundamentalist. We prayed together at study groups. We underwent a crisis of faith together, which brought an instant bond."

Damian was floored by his new friend's intellect. "One turning point in my life was when Daniel announced to me that the Holy Spirit is female," he says. "It connected to my Taoism, and made it real in a Christian sense. The elegance and beauty of this interpretation made it seem right."

The influence went both ways. Damian's Boulder-inflected Christianity had a different flavor from Daniel's conservatism. He introduced Daniel, who was now majoring in anthropology, to the writings of the Jesuit anthropologist Pierre Teilhard de Chardin, whose life work was an attempt to reconcile the theory of evolution with his faith that mankind existed for some divine purpose.

Teilhard, who had worked as a paleontologist excavating the remains of the prehistoric Peking man in the 1920s, matched

Darwin's wager and raised him a dollar. Not only had we evolved from cosmic dust to microorganisms to primates to Homo sapiens, but the process was not complete. Having only in the past several thousand years acquired consciousness, humans were now on the brink of another staggering advance. Teilhard suggested that all human thought mingled in a tangible substance around the earth that he called the "noosphere." To a visiting Martian, he postulated, "The first characteristic of our planet would be, not the blue of the seas or the green of the forests, but the phosphorescence of thought." And just as surely as fish developed gills and monkeys sprouted thumbs, this living organism of soul energy would evolve into something higher. "Are we not experiencing the first symptoms of an aggregation of a still higher order, the birth of some single centre from the convergent beams of millions of elementary centres dispersed over the thinking earth?" he asked. Eventually we would reach what he called "the Omega Point," and life on this earth would cease— just as all stars and planets die—but mankind would continue as some supremely conscious but as-yet-unfathomable life-form. "The noosphere . . . will reach its point of convergence—at the 'end of the world.'" This universal ascent to the heavens was, in Teilhard's mind, the return of Christ promised in the Bible.

If it sounds like the premise of a space-alien flick, that's because Teilhard's cosmic evolution was devoured and regurgitated by a generation of sci-fi writers. But in his prediction of a new era of evolved existence, Teilhard unknowingly built a bridge between fundamentalism and the New Age. The noosphere rising to the Omega Point wasn't all that different from John Darby's Sixth Dispensation, in which Christ returned and led the righteous into the Millennium. It was oddly similar to the promised New Age, too—specifically the Age of Aquarius that we are said to be entering due to realignment of distant stars, ushering in a two-thousand-year period of enlightenment that presumably improves upon the current Age of Pisces, characterized largely by greed, lust, gluttony, wrath, sloth, envy, and pride.

As he discussed with Damian the possibility that evolution was not the repudiation but the logical outcome of Christ's teaching, Daniel realized that being a man of science didn't prevent him from being a man of faith. Damian initiated Daniel into his circle of friends, Boulder natives who were looking for a more intense connection to the sacred than their churches could offer. Inspired by Jesus's embrace of the downtrodden, these suburban teenagers would befriend homeless people on the Boulder Mall and bring them to coffee hour at their churches. "I believed everybody should be welcome, including gay people, and smelly people," says Rebecca Mullen, who after high school had volunteered in Mother Teresa's convent in the South Bronx. When Daniel joined this group, their Christianity was edging toward the mystical.

"I was moving away from fundamentalism, into Buddhism and Sufi," says Dawn Larson, who was a CU sophomore when she met Daniel. "It was an ideal time to hook up with Dan: the long mystical talks for hours, his idea about the Holy Spirit."

On a typical Saturday night, this group of seekers might hike to a lake and pass around a bottle of wine. But unlike other undergraduates of their era, instead of breaking out the weed and mushrooms, they would sit in silent meditation and prayer, basking in nature's beauty, then regrouping for esoteric musing, usually with Daniel at the helm. "He's a master at understanding philosophical concepts and different paradigms, and being able to talk to people using their own lens and vocabulary," Larson says.

"There was an ethereal quality about him, a feeling like he wasn't completely attached to the earth," Mullen says. "Probably none of us were. We were all looking for some alternative to the spiritual conventions that were in front of us."

One of the concepts that Daniel wrestled with was time itself. Vine Deloria Jr., a CU professor and American Indian scholar, writes in *God Is Red*, "Christians see creation as the beginning event of a linear time sequence in which a divine plan is worked out, the conclusion of the sequence being an act of destruction bringing the world to an end." But the American Indian religions Suelo was studying were organized around space, not time. Deloria cites the Navajo creation myth as an example. "There is no doubt in any Navajo's mind that these particular mountains are the mountains where it all took place. No one can say when the creation story of the Navajo happened, but everyone is fairly certain *where* the emergence took place." Suddenly Daniel's lifelong belief in the impending Rapture seemed not God's truth but a cultural construct. Eastern religions, with their eternal cycles of reincarnation, echoed the cosmology of American Indian accounts, which suggested that time traveled not in a line but a circle.

Which is not to say that Daniel was drifting far from his roots. He and some friends from Intervarsity started their own Bible study at an off-campus house where Daniel rented a room. One of the core members was Tim Frederick, a shy computer science major whose Lutheran upbringing in Casper, Wyoming—his father managed the Sears outlet—rendered Daniel's itinerant childhood cosmopolitan by comparison. Tim was more square than

Damian and Dawn and Rebecca, but he was nonetheless drawn to Daniel's inquiries.

"I was always a geek who thought about the world in terms of science and technology," Frederick says. "Dan would bring me into the world of religion and philosophy." Frederick was attracted to the absence of judgment in the impromptu study group. Unlike what he had experienced in his traditional church, this was a group of people with large differences—Catholic, Lutheran, fundamentalist, charismatic—who still respected and listened to one another, and formed strong friendships. The chemistry was good. "While Dan had profound insights, he could also be an amazing listener," says Frederick, "taking in the comments and finding ways to connect them to what he had discovered."

When I looked up Tim Frederick three decades later, in the summer of 2010, his conventional life appeared the antithesis of Suelo's. Tim has held the same job since college, as a systems administrator for a government agency. He and his family live in a clean home in a new subdivision in the suburbs of Boulder. He attends the Lutheran church. He dresses the part of a computer whiz, down to the short-sleeved dress shirt, pleated slacks, and white running shoes. Here, surely, was a man whose real-world challenges—holding a job, supporting a family, paying a mortgage—would have soured him, or at least distanced him, from Suelo's reckless yearning.

But Tim Frederick remains Suelo's devoted friend. He chose Suelo as best man at his wedding, and named his son Daniel. He allowed me to download some forty-five handwritten letters that Suelo wrote him over a period of ten years, spanning more than two hundred pages. "I've considered it to be an honor and a privilege to be an 'archivist' contributor to this book project," he wrote. When Suelo and I traveled through Colorado, Tim Frederick received us like royalty. He and his wife, along with a few other old friends, dished up one course of home-cooked food after another, everyone intent on Suelo's words as we discussed God, the church, suicide, morality. I felt like we were back at Bible study.

(Suelo in his tramp's getup struck an odd figure in the land of Dockers. As we navigated the impossibly smooth cul-de-sacs, he asked me to pull over so he could pluck some unused candles from a pile of junk on the curb with the trash cans.)

Tim Frederick struck me as about as genuine and decent as a fellow could be. The process of digging up the old letters had triggered a flood of memories, and he wrote Suelo a note that he copied to me:

> *As I've followed your writing and your blog, and vicariously enjoyed your travels and your journey through moneyless discovery, I can see how much has changed for you too, and how much you've grown.*
>
> *That first day at the Bible Study . . . I knew that you had a beautiful character that went beyond the label of "Christian" or of any of the denominations we all represented. It was refreshing at the time to know such a person after I had struggled with Church of Christ on campus, and other situations where people were more concerned about making me who I wasn't rather than letting their own selves be known. I saw that strength of character in Ecuador through your struggles there, and through your very rough time afterwards. That character never changed—in fact it grew, and you were able to point out beautiful things even in the midst of your own despair.*

. . .

AT THE SAME time that Suelo's Christian faith was expanding, he was suffering the crisis that would eventually break it. Delving deeper into the feminine side of Christianity, he began battling with the most unwelcome biological urges. Daniel dated plenty of girls, but when it came time for the first kiss, he would freeze. "My heart would go pitter-patter from fear," he says, "and the girls would think it was attraction."

His closest friend in the dorms was a tomboy named Robin. They were both somewhat androgynous, he with his smooth face and delicate figure, she with short hair and baggy clothes. The two were inseparable, mutually infatuated, yet they didn't touch. "It seemed inappropriate to both of us," Suelo remembers. He wanted to believe his lack of libido was appropriate, given the prohibition on sex before marriage. As Valentine's Day approached, two girls on the hall teased him. "Have you kissed Robin yet?" They giggled. "Aren't you going to buy her flowers?" The thought disgusted him, but he succumbed to the pressure. *Maybe I am in love with Robin,* he told himself. In a burst of resolve, he bought a bouquet of roses and a box of chocolates, and knocked on her door. She looked at the gifts in horror. "She was pretending to enjoy it," he remembers. "After that it was really hard to be friends with her. Very embarrassing. We finally got over that and got back to our old selves."

One day the pair was out on the Boulder Mall when a flamboyantly pretty man sashayed up to Daniel, patted his butt, and whispered, "Aren't you cute!" Daniel, who had lived twenty years without fighting or cursing, shoved him off. "Get the hell away from me!" he screamed, his heart pounding. After he calmed down, he began to wonder what had been so frightening. He remembers thinking: *What am I afraid of? Not of him, but of what's in me.*

At Bible study, he had found himself locking eyes with a boy across the room, fixed in a hypnotic, breathless stare. "The flame was there," he remembers. "We went camping all the time. We'd pretend like we were wrestling, and had our hands on each other a lot, but neither of us would admit it. It's comical looking back on it."

Daniel's upbringing did not allow him to believe that his desires were natural, or right. They were the work of the devil, and he kept them under wraps. Fortunately, celibacy before marriage was expected, and as long as Daniel remained unmarried, nobody would interpret his virginity as a lack of attraction to women. He hid his true self from his female friends, many of whom fell for him. Dawn Larson, who at nineteen had almost no dating experience of her own, often found herself paired up with Daniel.

"He was a cutie, a sexy guy, attractive in that natural sort of way," Larson says today. "He wasn't afraid of emotions, but he was also very strong. That's a hard blend to find."

Unable to contain her attraction, Larson told Daniel that she'd never felt such a strong connection with someone. Daniel blinked and said, "We're all connected in God's grace." They never spoke of it again.

Daniel maintained his strongest affection for male friends. "One day Daniel said something extremely attractive," Damian Nash remembers. "He wanted a friend he could be together with and not have to talk. Everything would be understood. Almost telepathic. Over the years he has groomed me into that."

Celibacy and theology, however, could not prevent Daniel

from falling in love. His first crush, alas, was on his straight best friend. "I was a Christian evangelical, a virgin, as naive as a young man can be," says Nash. "The line between eros and agape was blurred." But even as both men sensed their friendship was beyond the norm, Daniel could not admit that his attraction was physical, and neither could Damian perceive it.

By the time he graduated, Daniel Shellabarger had won the friendship and admiration of many whose paths he crossed. But as he set out into the world in the summer of 1985 with his degree, he was distraught. His treatise on the feminine nature of God made for scintillating chats in classrooms and Bible study, but the manuscript itself was a mess—the incoherent passions of a college sophomore, on a subject at once too deep in biblical esoterica for secular readers yet downright heretical to most evangelicals. A few years later he burned the thing. He departed the academy wondering how to put his beliefs into practice, less sure about his place in the world than when he started. The predictions of his family's congregation were proving true: Boulder had rattled his fundamentalism.

. . .

SUELO'S RELIGIOUS TRANSFORMATION in college was accompanied by a political awakening. This was the eighties, and contrary to the national conservative trend, in academia leftist professors were successfully challenging the supremacy of the canon produced largely by white men of privilege. The narrative of the West as enlightened protector of freedoms lost ground to a vision of the West as colonial exploiter and oppressor of women and minorities. Departments of African-American, American

Indian, and women's studies cropped up in universities to grant institutional validity to these ideas.

Suelo was particularly influenced by the writings of American Indians like Black Elk, John Lame Deer, and Vine Deloria Jr. These thinkers confirmed the beliefs he'd first contemplated in South America: that the money system was rigged to benefit the wealthy, and the people who had the least were the most willing to share. White Americans, writes Lame Deer in *Lame Deer: Seeker of Visions*, "are also wagging their fingers at us when we have a give-away feast. What they are trying to tell us is that poor people can't afford to be generous. But we hold onto our outhan, our give-aways, because they help us to remain Indians. All the big events in our lives—birth and death, joy and sadness—can be occasions for give-aways. We don't believe in a family getting wealthy through inheritance. Better to give away a dead person's belongings. That way he, or she, will be remembered." This sort of thinking, combined with the liberation theology he was learning from Dr. Mahan, convinced Suelo that the way to put his beliefs into practice was to work with poor people in the Third World.

In 1987 he joined the Peace Corps and was sent to Ecuador. He was twenty-six, an innocent with a head full of theology. Of course idealists with liberal-arts degrees were not rare in the Peace Corps, but fundamentalist Christians were. For most of his two years in South America, Daniel kept a daily journal, copies of which he meticulously transcribed by hand on lined paper and sent to his parents in thirty-page installments, rich with detail and tender with introspection. The first letter described crying the entire flight from Grand Junction to Denver, then reaching an epiphany on the way to Miami:

As we passed over the clouds I started thinking about my destina-
tion, and for the first time since I started my journey I felt butter-
flies in my stomach. "Am I doing the right thing?" I thought. And
just as those thoughts ran through my head I received my answer—
the answer God always seems to give me when I need reassurance,
no matter what time of year it is or where I am: I saw a rainbow.
Yes, a rainbow right there above the clouds. God's promise of reas-
surance to mankind. God's sign of peace, and His Covenant
between Heaven & Earth.

What's absent from Suelo's letters is the tone that would
become emblematic of his generation: irony. His reports range
from the aw-shucks delight of a rube ("The bananas are delicious
here!") to the wide-eyed bedazzlement of an innocent abroad
("The churches are especially beautiful, intricately carved on the
outside, towering in spires toward the sky, and full of paintings
and gold-plated sculptures") to the stirrings of conscience of a
son of empire: "It is hard to tell how much of the coldness is due
to the communist propaganda against 'Yankees.' It is also true
that there are many foreign corporations & oil companies totally
exploiting the people here."

Suelo had none of the jaded worldliness of his peers. His fellow Peace Corps volunteer Corinne Pochitaloff says, "He was a
devout and spiritual young man, more contemplative of a person
than the rest of us. He was moved and distressed by the state of
affairs of the Amazon and I remember feeling that he would
take action in the future. He was a force of good."

What I find most powerful is his earnest wrestling with
faith. He wrote to his parents: "We have talked about how the
Indians from North America to South America have been

pushed around and massacred through the centuries and how these facts are conveniently left out of our history books in public schools both in the USA and here in Latin America. We must pray that the Love of Christ covers the multitudes of sins on our hands so that people will no longer notice our evil but our good."

The next blow to his religious convictions came when he and Corinne went to visit a missionary who knew Daniel's family. Envisioning some swashbuckler in a jungle hut surrounded by natives in loincloths, Suelo was alarmed by what he discovered.

"He was in this huge suburban house surrounded by barbed wire to keep people out," Suelo remembers. "He talked about what he was doing with the indigenous people in the jungle, mostly the Huaorani and the Quechua." The missionary, with the blessing of the Ecuadoran government, had gone into the cattle business, shipping a herd from North America. He had brokered a deal with his converts: if they raised and fed his cattle, the government would grant them a plot of jungle, and the converts would be entitled to keep every other generation of calves. The alternating generation would be added to the American's herd.

"Before we came here the Indians had the whole family sleeping in one bed, and they didn't have radios or TVs," boasted the missionary. "Now the Christian Indians are the richest in the jungle."

"This is why governments all over the world love missionaries—they civilize people and get them into the money system," Suelo observes now, but at the time he was flabbergasted. What of Jesus's teaching his followers to give up possessions? "And suddenly it dawned on me: if you were going to call something Antichrist, this would be it. The people who were promoting this so-called Christianity are really Antichrist."

What's more, with each acre of land doled out to ranching, more jungle was clear-cut. And after just a few years of grazing, the land was unusable, turned into desert.

"What about the jungle?" Daniel asked.

"It's infinite," said the missionary. "If you're up in a plane, look at the Amazon. It goes on for miles."

Daniel took a scenic flight over the Amazon. "It looked like Paul Bunyan had taken a razor blade to it."

On the way back to Quito, Suelo juggled the contradictions. On the one hand, the missionary was doing some tangible good work for the Indians—fighting for their legal rights, promoting their education. On the other hand, introducing them to the money system didn't seem to help. "There was no poverty in the jungle until they introduced money, and all the sudden there's poverty," he says. "And all the diseases that come with it. And you look at people and they're not happy. They have all these goods, and they're unhappy."

Suelo's doubts deepened as he began his assignment in the remote Andean village of El Hato, population three hundred. Armed with an identification card with the title of "Health Extensionist," Suelo arrived ready to teach first aid and nutrition.

"Usted es doctor?" said the villagers. You're a doctor?

"Not exactly," he replied, struggling in broken Spanish to explain *extensionista de salud*.

The first order of business was to rent a home. Suelo had envisioned a dirt-floor hut just like the natives had. But the villagers wanted to rent him the concrete box of an abandoned health clinic. *"Usted es doctor,"* they insisted.

Whether or not they believed his protestations, the locals made clear that the only edifice for rent was the clinic. And so

Daniel moved in. In a chain of events that could not have been better scripted by a writer of television sitcoms, as soon as he unshuttered the doors, the patients arrived in droves, having walked miles over mountain passes, and presented Daniel with their phlegm, sprains, and rashes—ready to barter milk and chickens for his services. After a few months of pointless protest, Suelo decided that since he couldn't beat them, he might as well join them. He traveled to Quito, and with his meager stipend and his mysterious ID card, loaded up at the pharmacy on antibiotics, aspirin, acetaminophen, Benadryl, and epinephrine, as well as a handy paperback written by a former Peace Corps volunteer, *Donde No Hay Doctor*, on how to administer care when there's no doctor for miles. By the end of his term, Suelo had treated innumerable maladies, sent a few serious cases to the nearest clinic, and armed with nothing more than clean towels, a pail of hot water, and *Donde No Hay Doctor*, delivered three healthy babies.

"They wanted to walk around and, like, do stuff," Suelo says of the laboring mothers he encountered. "So I let them. I recommended that they squat, and they did, and the baby slid right out into my hands. The last one I did, the baby almost hit the floor."

Medical triumphs notwithstanding, Suelo felt a deepening disillusionment with Western efforts—both religious and secular—to improve lives in Ecuador. A woman he'd befriended at the clinic required surgery that would cost two hundred dollars, but the family was poor, chronically in debt, and the husband earned only a dollar a day. Suelo wrote to his college friend Tim Frederick, asking him to take up a collection at his church in Boulder, hoping the congregation would send the cash immediately, without any questions or board meetings. "That's the way Christianity should be," he wrote, "the way Jesus taught it."

Although the money arrived as hoped, Suelo continued to feel that the system of delivering charity was flawed beyond his ability to fix it. He wrote to Tim Frederick, "I feel very strongly, now more than ever, that any influence I have on these people should be on the individual level—helping and sharing knowledge on a one-on-one level, with my life, not with set programs."

Meanwhile, his sexual confusion raged. Daniel continued to strike up close friendships with women, partly because he genuinely liked them, and partly because he hoped Miss Right might marshal his hormones to march to the correct drummer. He reported in a letter to Tim Frederick, "I have had most of my fellowship with a girl, Corinne, who used to be involved in Intervarsity and is a Lutheran. We played 'hooky' from training one day and spent the day in Quito going from one cathedral to another, praying and talking about the mysteries of the Universe. I was on a spiritual high for days afterward."

Corinne, who went on to a career in Foreign Service, was also on a high, but perhaps of a different nature. She recalls Daniel as "very handsome, but not flirtatious, or trivial," and remembers thinking: *What's up with this guy? It's weird we spend so much time together and it's not leading toward romance. He doesn't seem to be interested.*

Daniel rationalized his indifference in a letter to Tim Frederick: "I told her there was nothing noble in my lack of interest in a male/female relationship. I just had no instinctual desire to be involved with a woman, so I had to turn to a higher goal—my theology." He had acquired a sort of holy pride in his skittishness. When he got news that a friend was getting married, he joked to Tim, "They're betraying us and our Celibate Club. Who's next? The Pope?" But even as his attraction to men roiled, he couldn't bring himself to broach the real issue with his best friends. "I have deep-hurting problems that I would like to share with you," he wrote to Tim, promising to do so in the next letter, but he didn't.

Finally the pot boiled over. In the second year of his Peace Corps term, Daniel found himself drinking with the locals at a party in his mountain village. He locked eyes with a man on the dance floor. Daniel felt like he was being swept away. They danced closer and closer. "The next thing I know I put my hand on his back," he says. "I felt this mutual attraction. I was just sober enough to control myself. I thought: 'I'm in a different culture that doesn't accept this.'"

Daniel stumbled home alone. He could no longer deny how he felt. But instead of jumping into the arms of the first available man, his first act as an openly gay man was to sit down and write a letter to his parents.

"I am gay," he wrote. "Homosexual. Have been since birth and there is no way to change it. I believe it's the same thorn in the flesh that the Apostle Paul had, only he was satisfied in asking God only 3 times to remove it while I've begged God thousands of times to take it away."

Daniel mailed the letter and felt relief and joy wash over him. He came out to Corinne, and their friendship blossomed again. "Now I can say I'm glad I'm gay and it's no longer something I'm gonna hide," he wrote to Tim. "I can finally say I love myself."

The elation of sending his coming-out letter to his parents began to erode as weeks with no reply stretched into months. "I thought they had disowned me," he remembers. Then a telegram arrived from Peace Corps headquarters in Quito. *Urgent. Call parents*. Phone service was unreliable in El Hato, so Daniel packed a bag and took the bus to Quito, assuming somebody had died. He rang his parents.

"Did you get my letter?" he asked.

"Yes," said Dad. Silence.

Finally Mom said, "I want you to come home."

Daniel later learned that the letter had been damaged and delayed for months in the Ecuadorian mail. The tatters that finally arrived were largely illegible, except for the part where he said he was gay. His parents had reported to the Peace Corps that Daniel was mentally ill, and needed to be shipped home. His bosses, accustomed to such panicked calls from parents, made sure that Daniel called home, and then allowed him to return to his village.

Having been declared insane by his parents, however, he began to feel that all the things that he'd believed in—family, religion, the Peace Corps—were meaningless. Where was God in all of this? For the first time in his life, he understood how someone could become an atheist. To make matters worse, he was slipping into what he would later learn was clinical depression. As Daniel teetered on the verge of despair, an unlikely event pushed him over the edge.

·   ·   ·

ONE DAY HE and some friends went blueberry picking in the mountains. Suelo gorged himself, not only on the sweet, chalky blueberries but on a similar berry, shinier and more bitter. When his friend saw what he was doing, she said, "I don't think you're supposed to eat those."

"What are they?"

"Morideros." The name was a pun on the words for "dog bite" and "death."

Later that night Suelo ran into some other friends, who invited him in for dinner. He accepted, then suddenly found that his brain wasn't working. "I started to feel like I couldn't think sequentially. I couldn't speak Spanish hardly. Incoherent things were coming out of my mouth." A headache descended, and pleading illness, Suelo left alone.

"I felt like everything was alive," he says. "I could feel the earth breathing. Everything was in pain and I felt like crying." He approached a cow tied to a post. The tether allowed the animal to walk no more than a tiny circle. "The rope was chafing her nose, blood coming down," he says. "It seemed so wrong. I almost let the cow go. Everything seemed horrifying."

Things got worse. His head was splitting. He looked at a book and couldn't decipher the words. He tried to speak but no syllables arrived. Daniel could think of no explanation other than he was losing his mind. He ran into another friend, and when he told her what he'd eaten that day, she gasped. "I think people die from those!"

Suelo raced home and locked himself in his apartment, oscillating between panic and grief. "Everything was spinning and my head felt like it was going to burst. My emotions were on a roller coaster. I found myself crying, thinking I was going to die."

When morning arrived, he was still alive. A few days later, thinking it was over, Suelo smoked some marijuana—a habit his fellow Peace Corps volunteers had introduced. Now the nightmare returned, only worse. "I ended up in the fetal position, twitching, convulsions . . . I was thinking I might die in this room by myself, in Ecuador, thinking about my family. What a stupid way to die." The drug induced a series of hallucinations: "I had this vision of a cross. I'm on the equator, this is where the tectonic plates come together, I'm at the center of this cross. Jesus on a cross was in my vision. I was saying: 'My God, my God, why have you forsaken me?'" He realized that all the universe was a single being—and yet, paradoxically, each of us is utterly alone.

His vision would stick with him for years. "I felt like I was in eternity, being reincarnated over and over and over, and there was no way out." The feeling of eternal suffering is common enough during bad trips, but for Suelo it was particularly terrifying. All his life he had believed in heaven. Finally he had tapped into the eternal—but it wasn't joy and forgiveness. It was misery and suffering. It wasn't heaven, it was hell.

By morning, the bell jar had descended. The creeping depression was now acute. He lost his appetite, and his stomach was chronically upset. His budding sex drive withered. He didn't want to get out of bed. He lost interest in administering first aid and in the entire purpose of the Peace Corps, and began counting the days until his stint ended.

After the poisoning, his letters adopted a disturbed tone. "My head is going to explode," he warned in one, then made a bitter pun on the Peace Corps: "No body can live in peace, in reality, until it's a corpse." He complained, "The good people always get screwed, that's the story of life . . . from the beginning." And in questioning his mental health, he hinted at the path that lay before him: "I may have sacrificed my sanity but have gained something indescribable that is eternal."

. . .

WHEN DANIEL RETURNED to Colorado in 1990, the depression worsened. Although he'd pined for a culture where being gay was acceptable, he found the scene in Denver soulless. The guys he met at bars were queeny and materialistic, only interested in partying and having sex—nothing like the male friends he'd made in college, so vulnerable in their longing and contemplation.

His coming-out to Damian was profoundly awkward. Upon arriving home, the two friends went for a drive, and Daniel broke the news. Damian was silent, doing the math.

"Does that mean you've had feelings toward me?"

Daniel fidgeted, looked away. Finally: "Yeah."

It just didn't make sense to Damian. He loved Daniel like a brother, as much as he loved anyone. But he didn't have *those* kind of feelings. "I spent the next few years searching for signs of gayness," he says. "There was a part of me that wanted to be gay, just because I loved Daniel so much. Unfortunately, I came up negative. In those years I wanted to hump almost every woman I saw."

The discomfort of his friends was nothing compared to the reaction of his parents. On his first visit home, his mother was unable to speak to him about what he'd written. His father took him to dinner—the first time the two of them had gone to a restaurant alone. As they ate, Dick Shellabarger recounted how he had always loved his children unconditionally, as Christians were supposed to.

"Even if you go out and murder someone, I'll still love you," he said. "But this time God threw me a curveball. Because actually there was one sin I thought was worse than murder: homosexuality.

So this has been a big test. You have to know the culture I came from, my generation. They'd go out and beat up gays."

And then, for the first time, Daniel watched his towering cowboy of a father break down and weep. Dick Shellabarger was sure that some aberration he himself had committed had caused Daniel to be gay. Maybe he should have taken him to more ball games, maybe Mother should have breast-fed for longer. And Daniel found himself in the peculiar position of leaning forward, telling his father everything was going to be okay.

His parents' disapproval was just one more symptom of his world in collapse. Clinging to the remnants of his beliefs in social justice, Suelo settled in Denver and went to work as a counselor at a homeless shelter. The job soured from the start. The place was operated by a nominally Christian outfit, but while it didn't preach to the residents, the director was prone to belittling them. She would humiliate them, yell at them in front of others for being dirty, poor, stupid, unable to make their own beds. Suelo discussed this behavior with a coworker, and they decided to bring it up at the next staff meeting.

"I think the way you treat the clients is abusive," Daniel sputtered. "It's a dishonor to your religion—if you consider yourself a Christian." He warned that if things didn't change, he was prepared to take the complaint further. He scanned the table for support, but his colleagues were looking down at their notebooks. The director didn't say a word, she just glared. Nobody would even meet her eyes, much less raise their voice.

She never addressed Suelo's complaints. She merely began to reduce his hours. The abuse continued. If she found the shelter messy, she'd start yelling, working herself into a rage until finally she was hurling clothes and newspapers across the room.

Residents and employees cast their eyes at the floor. Everything came to head in a scene straight out of *Oliver Twist*.

After lunch, a resident asked the director for an extra carton of milk.

The staff knew that locked in the kitchen were dozens of donated milk cartons, approaching their expiration date. Yet the director turned on the resident in a fury. "This milk," she said, trembling, "is for the *babies*! And you're so damn selfish that you'd drink it *all* if we let you. The answer is no! You should be ashamed for even asking."

That night Daniel had the graveyard shift. The director told him to lock the dining-hall doors so the residents couldn't leave until they'd finished their chores. Daniel considered the order. Not only was it humiliating to treat the homeless like prisoners— it was unethical. What if there were a fire? Defying her orders, he left the doors unlocked, and spent the night penning a furious letter of resignation. He wrote about the door-locking and declared, "I can no longer carry through with your wishes."

When he was finished, he considered what to do with the letter. It needed a wider audience than the director, who would doubtlessly shred the thing and be done with it. In a fit of moral resolve, Suelo made copies and tacked them up throughout the shelter, his own version of Luther's 95 Theses. The homeless had found their advocate! One of them collected fifty signatures on the manifesto. Another delivered the letter to the Denver newspapers.

The hounds of hell were unleashed. The shelter's parent organization launched an investigation, and revealed that the director had been running some sort of black-market milk ring— auctioning off the extras and pocketing the money. She was fired, and for a brief moment Daniel was a hero.

No good deed goes unpunished. The investigation's other finding was that the old barracks was filled with radiation. There was no option but to raze it. And now dozens of freshly empowered residents were turned out onto the street. And a dozen social workers—including Suelo—were sacked. "Now look what you've done," his coworkers hissed, packing their photos and staplers into cardboard boxes.

Next Suelo took a job at Travelers Aid, a charity that helps needy people in times of transition. The results were similar. On a typical day, a down-and-out hobo shuffled into his cubicle and wanted a bus ticket to Phoenix.

"There's construction work down there," said the man.

"We can help you with that," Suelo said, withdrawing a clipboard with a four-page questionnaire. "We'll just need a little information."

Daniel recorded the guy's stats. Jerry Banks was forty-nine years old, twice divorced, Vietnam vet, worked odd jobs and manual labor, unemployed for two years since he got out of jail for a DUI. Now he'd lost his license, and it was hard to get a construction job when you couldn't drive yourself to the site. He stayed in cheap motels whenever he got a check from the VA, but mostly it was homeless shelters or camping under an overpass.

"Where will you be staying in Phoenix?"

"I've asked the maid to get the house all cleaned up for me."

Daniel looked up from his clipboard.

"Is there an address for that?"

"If I had a house in Phoenix," said Banks, leaning in close, "I probably wouldn't be in here trying to get a Greyhound ticket."

"Right. Sorry. But to process this application I need to write in the address of where you'll be staying. Do you have any family there?"

"My sister's in Tempe."

"Great. What's her name?"

Banks said her name, and Daniel entered it on the form.

"Address?"

"I haven't seen my sister in eleven years."

"Okay. Fine. We'll make this work." In the box for "Address" Daniel wrote "302 Main Street, Phoenix, AZ" and for "Phone" he scribbled his own home number with an Arizona area code.

"Moving on," said Daniel. "Do you have a job lined up in Phoenix?"

"Gotta get there first."

"Right," said Daniel. "I just need to write something here."

"Hanging drywall isn't the kind of business where they hire a Bekins van to bring you to town."

"Can you give me a name?" said Daniel. "Any name will do."

Banks just looked at him. Then he fished his wallet out of his pocket, pulled out a scrap of paper, and scrutinized it at arm's length.

"Did you know that the average Somalian survives on twelve cents per day?" said Jerry Banks.

"Excuse me?"

"Twelve cents a day. Sometimes in the library I'll find some factoid like that and I just have to write it down. Blows my mind." He opened his wallet so that Daniel could look inside. Dozens of soiled paper scraps clung together in the musty leather. The man flipped the card over in his hand. "Here's the name of a guy who runs a drywall outfit. I got his number from

my sponsor. When I called him he said they were always looking for workers and to call back when I got to town."

Daniel jotted down the name and number. He was required
to call the employer to verify that they intended to hire the traveler. That way, Travelers Aid didn't foot the bill for hobos merely
joyriding across the country.

"I'll give him a call right now and we can finalize this," Daniel said. "Would you take a seat in the waiting room?"

The client lifted himself out of the chair with a groan and
shuffled out of the office. Daniel dialed the number and a gruff
voice answered.

"I'm calling for Manny Velazquez . . ."

"Speaking."

"This is Daniel Shellabarger with Travelers Aid in Denver,
Colorado. I'm calling to verify an offer of employment for our
client, Gerald Banks."

"Who?"

"Daniel Shellabarger," he repeated. *S-H-E-L-L—*"

"And you want a job?"

"I'm calling on behalf of a client, Gerald Banks. He says he's
intending to work for you."

"I get a lot of calls," said the man.

"Do you remember a Jerry Banks?"

"That sounds familiar. What do you mean, he's your client?"

"I work with the Denver office of Travelers Aid."

"What is this guy—a vagrant?"

"Well, no," Suelo stammered. "He's a member of an under-
served population with limited social mobility and—"

"I told Hank to quit giving out my number to deadbeats."

Suelo pressed his pencil onto the application form until the lead broke. "Can you confirm an offer of employment made to Gerald Banks for September of this year?"

"I don't hire those type of people," said Manny Velazquez. "I've tried it and it never works. I make a donation every month to St. Vincent de Paul. I got nothing against those people, I just don't want them on my crew. Hey, my other line's ringing, so I gotta go."

Click. Daniel set down the phone. His shirt clung damply to his spine. He reached for his water cup but it was empty. He looked at the forms on his clipboard. In the past he had fudged little details like phone numbers and addresses and had got the payments processed. But today he was going to have to falsify the entire document. If anyone audited, he'd be fired. And wasn't all this paperwork a bunch of bullshit anyway? If Jerry Banks had a job and a home, he wouldn't need Travelers Aid. The whole bureaucracy was set up to cover its own ass and write clean expense reports—not to actually help anyone in need. He hated it all. He felt like a fraud. After spending eight hours a day in this office, being paid to be kind to someone, he found that at the end of the day, he hated homeless people. When he saw them on his block as he plodded toward his apartment, he wanted to tell them to fuck off and get out of his way. His job was nothing more than glorified prostitution. He was paid to be helpful. It wasn't coming from his heart. He was just doing it for money. And now he had to lie and commit forgery and risk getting fired just to actually help another human being— although best as he could tell, he'd just ruined Jerry Banks's chances of getting a job.

He tore the papers off the clipboard, crumpled them into a ball, and chucked it into the wastepaper basket. Then he pulled out his own wallet and counted his money. Two twenties and three ones. He called Mr. Banks back into the office.

"Great news, Jerry," Daniel said. "Everything was approved and you're all set to go. Here's forty-three dollars—that should be enough for the fare to Arizona."

Jerry's eyes lit up and he smiled as he collected the money. "Do I need to sign anywhere, or something like that?"

"You're all set. Have a safe trip."

More and more, Suelo sensed that the whole enterprise of professional charity was flawed. Instead of counting beans in this dehumanizing system, why couldn't we just help our neighbors directly?

More than a year since his return from the Peace Corps, all his efforts to do good were backfiring. In 1991 his friends persuaded him to get counseling, but the therapist was so young and inexperienced that as a matter of intellectual pride Suelo convinced her that nothing was wrong. She gave him a clean bill of mental health. His roommate took him to a Bible study one night, on the topic of the parable of the Good Samaritan. But when the people at his table made some snide comments about Mormons—always the whipping boys for evangelicals—Suelo took the opportunity to rub their noses in their bigotry. He flipped open the Book of Luke and read furiously, substituting modern words for the archaic.

"'An *evangelical* happened to be going down the same road, and when he saw the man, he passed by on the other side,'" he said. "'So, too, a *fundamentalist*, when he came to the place and saw him, passed by on the other side. But a *Mormon*, as he traveled, came where the man was; and when he saw him, he took pity on him.'"

Everything was spiraling downward. Suelo was sleeping only an hour or two a night, lying breathlessly awake on his mattress, making an inventory of his multitude of miseries. And then one May night he bolted upright and dashed for the calendar. With a pencil he scratched off days and weeks. In three entire months, he calculated, he had been happy for precisely five minutes. There was no end to the eternal misery he had discovered in the poison berries.

Suddenly he knew the solution. When he was a child, his father had packed the family into the Beetle and driven them up the steep, treacherous road to Mount Evans. It's one of only two four-teeners in Colorado that you can drive to the top of. Daniel remembered the road, its hairpin switchbacks into deep gorges that dropped thousands of feet. There was a way to end this suffering.

.   .   .

AT THREE IN the morning, Suelo dresses and starts the sedan. He takes the highway into the Rockies, the same evergreen range where his father broke horses and courted his mother. He exits at the Mount Evans road and winds up into the mist. It's spring, and the asphalt is wet from the packs of dirty snow clinging to the mountainside. He knows his destination. He can picture it.

The road narrows and grows steeper. Now, with the black night turning gray, he can see an icy lake so far below it looks like a puddle. His is the only car on the road. *What kind of lunatic would be driving up Mount Evans at this hour?* he thinks, and gets a laugh out of that. He steers to the precipice and peers over. A quick drop-off, then a steep slope of boulders, the tips of wild grasses poking through the snow, then the big free fall, hundreds of feet down to the lake.

He makes a note of the spot. The shoulder is crumbling into the abyss, and steel girders prop it up. He drives to the pullout and turns around, preparing for a final approach. His heart leaps to his throat.

And then, as he points the wheel toward the edge, something emerges from the fog. It's an animal, two, three, more. Is he hallucinating again? No: it's a herd of mountain goats, with their knobby knees and white fur and spiked horns. The goats have descended the slope opposite the drop-off, and are making their way up the road. One approaches the car. Daniel rolls down the window. Man and beast look into each other's eyes. The goat has wet black compassionate eyes, two saucers of oil. And Daniel feels oddly comforted, as if the animal has given him permission to do what he's about to do.

He punches the gas. The car jerks toward the cliff. Daniel thinks: *If God has some purpose for me, then not even I can resist it.*

The rocks scrape beneath as he launches. Then blackness.

Part Two

6

. . .

Do not expect me to be a man in the worldly sense.

—Milarepa, eleventh-century Tibetan Buddhist saint

MAY 30, 1991. Daniel Shellabarger drives his car off a Colorado cliff toward certain death. Even viewed as a solitary event in a troubled life, it's a dramatic moment. Yet in the context of all that came next, the crash assumes almost supernatural importance. Instead of a series of disconnected episodes without clear purpose, Suelo's life begins to resemble an ordered fable, in which one scene leads irreversibly to the next, in which things happen for a reason.

The term for such a tale—in which the hero's journey and ultimate battle against the dragon is choreographed by fate—is myth. Suelo's quest to rid himself of money, when measured by modern yardsticks like politics and economics and psychology, just doesn't add up. People in the real world *don't behave like this*. The genre in which people wander for years in the desert, give up all worldly possessions, dwell in caves, and survive a series of near-death trials, is mythology.

"A hero ventures forth from the world of common day into a region of supernatural wonder," wrote Joseph Campbell in *The Hero with a Thousand Faces*, his 1949 exploration of religion and mythology that inspired, among other things, the heroic journey of Luke Skywalker. "Fabulous forces are there encountered and a decisive victory is won: the hero comes back from this mysterious adventure with the power to bestow boons on his fellow man."

Outlining the journey's three phases—Departure, Initiation, Return—Campbell proposes that a hero's "visions, ideas, and inspirations come pristine from the primary springs of human life and thought . . . not of the present, disintegrating society and psyche, but of the unquenched source through which society is reborn."

Suelo long struggled with the ordinary world. As a child, he believed that through faith in Jesus he would spend eternity in heaven, but early in adulthood he lost faith in God, and doubted the eternal. As a young man, he was mired in a world in which his admiration of the great heroes—Jesus, John the Baptist, the prophet Daniel—was met with the same reply: *We're living in different times now.* But Suelo did not accept that explanation. He demanded a life that emanated from more primary sources.

Then one day he was called to adventure. While innocently collecting berries in the woods, he ate the poisonous fruit, the *morideros.* "A blunder," writes Campbell, "apparently the merest chance—reveals an unsuspected world, and the individual is drawn into a relationship with forces that are not rightly understood."

Poisoned by the magical berries—"bites of death"—Suelo had his first true vision of the eternal. Much to his horror, it was

not a place where angels strummed harps. It was a place of
Christ nailed to the cross and never-ending suffering. It was
hell, and his path of Bible study and good deeds would never
lead him to heaven.

Is that reading a bit too much into a case of accidental poisoning? Couldn't Daniel have just as easily seen fairies and unicorns?
But blunders are not random, according to Campbell. "They are
the result of suppressed desires and conflicts," he writes. "They are
ripples on the surface of life, produced by unsuspected springs."
Suelo's vision of hell was already within him; the *morideros* presented themselves on the vine in order to make him see it.

Thus called to his quest, Suelo reacted by refusing it. He was
like Moses, who, when apprised of his task to free his people,
cried out, "O Lord, please send someone else to do it." Suelo's
method of refusing the call was to drive off a cliff.

And that's when he first experienced what Campbell calls
"Supernatural Aid." The car soared into the abyss but never
reached bottom. As if lifted by angels, Suelo found himself alive
on the side of the road. Helicoptered to a Denver hospital, he
emerged virtually unscathed. He could not refuse the call to
adventure. Fate would not allow it. He cursed God, bitter that
the Father would force him to endure an existence that, like it
or not, would last forever. The purpose of his quest, then, was
becoming clear: to transform this life from hell into heaven.

The year was 1991. The economy was in recession, and our
hero was a thirty-one-year-old social worker with a case of sui-
cidal depression—trapped in the belly of the beast. A year
passed. Everywhere he looked, the world was ugly. He wanted
to get away from its materialism and headaches and phoniness.
He wanted to start fresh in some place that was uncluttered by

modernity, where man's folly was cast into puny relief by nature, where a man might indeed believe that these times are no different from those of the ancient heroes.

Like many seekers before him, he didn't exactly choose the tiny speck on the map. The speck chose him. His friend Damian Nash had moved to Utah, and invited Daniel to join him in a busted dust-swept uranium outpost. The town, an oasis amid golden cliffs, just happened to have been named after the biblical land along the River Jordan, the same river across which Moses led his people into the Promised Land, the same one where John the Baptist cleansed the soul of Jesus.

To ring in the 1993 New Year, Suelo typed a note to his friends:

> Daniel Shellabarger has boycotted his native ¿civilization? and receded into the primitive desertlands of the Anasazi for a life of disciplined vision-quest.

And then in smaller font:

> and/or fun-in-the-sun and debauchery.

With that, Daniel set out through the desert, crossed the rushing waters into Moab, and began his journey.

7

. . .

Let right deeds be thy motive, not the fruit which comes
from them.

—The Bhagavad Gita

A CONFESSION: I like getting my annual Social Security statement. Each year when it arrives, I tear open the envelope eagerly,
to *see how I've done.* The numbers—the list of my earnings for
every year I have worked, and the benefits to my survivors should
I die this year—tell a version of my life story. And the story is
largely optimistic. They show a gradual increase in my taxable
earnings, from a mere sixty dollars the year I turned sixteen,
soaring into triple digits during my tenure as a work-study dish-
washer, hovering around ten grand in my decade as a seasonal
river guide and underemployed drifter, then finally, in the past
couple of years, as I was paid to write and teach, ramming
through the poverty line into the realm of respectability.

Daniel Suelo gets a Social Security statement each year, too,
delivered to his parents' house. When he showed it to me, the
exquisite column of zeros from 2001 to 2010 sent a shudder
down my spine. That numeric representation of nothingness

made him seem so fragile, as if the slightest breeze could whisk Daniel into oblivion. But then I felt something like elation. According to the tax man's definition of work—the tasks you do in exchange for money—these numbers told Suelo's story of liberation. He had freed himself.

The Social Security statements, however, tell only one side of our work story. As much as Americans gripe about wanting to take this job and shove it, work provides rewards beyond money that are difficult to find elsewhere: the satisfaction of competence and achievement, the bond of a community, the pride of recognition and acclaim. What's more, many don't accept the strictly monetary definition of work because it excludes a host of unpaid activities like parenting, volunteering, and writing poems.

Some people reject the American concept of work altogether. "I didn't want a steady job in an office or a factory," writes Lame Deer, the Sioux medicine man. "I thought myself too good for that, not because I was stuck up but because any human being is too good for that kind of no-life, even white people. I trained myself to need and want as little as could be so that I wouldn't have to work except when I felt like it. That way I could get along fine with plenty of spare time to think, to ask, to learn, to listen, and to count coup on the girls."

And then there's Thoreau. "For many years I was self-appointed inspector of snow-storms and rain-storms," he claimed, "and did my duty faithfully." For him and for many who've followed in his tracks, work is the tasks that give life meaning, regardless of whether money is earned.

Suelo, with his philosophical opposition to gainful employment, still seeks the rewards of meaningful vocation. He just finds them in different ways. He certainly does the kind of work of which Thoreau and Lame Deer might approve. "I watched a daddy longlegs bug crawl out into sun from the cave," he wrote one crisp February morning. "I decided to follow him." Suelo was impressed by how the spider, with no possessions nor even any food, seemed to wander without destination. "I must have followed him for four hours."

Suelo tends to speak of his vocation in more abstract terms:

I'm employed by the universe. Since everywhere I go is the universe, I am always secure. Life has flourished for billions of years like this. I never knew such security before I gave up money. Wealth is what we are dependent upon for security. My wealth never leaves me. Do you think Bill Gates is more secure than I?

But the truth is, Suelo does a great deal of what would more conventionally be recognized as work—he just does it without pay.

Damian Nash, in the wake of a 2009 newspaper article that elicited attacks on Suelo as a freeloader, itemized the ways in which Suelo "adds value" when he visits. Among Suelo's contributions—in addition to the fresh watermelons—are pet watching, tree pruning, car repairing, and spiritual counseling. "I'll let the accountants of human value put a price tag on all of the above," wrote Nash. "My estimate is that he gave back at least twice the value he received."

Removing money from the equation, Suelo's use of his time might be seen not as adventure or creative expression, but as unpaid labor for projects he deems worthwhile. The three months perched atop that hemlock tree on the Oregon coast were an endeavor to prevent it from being logged. Painting murals for Moab's Youth Garden Project is an act of service. When he volunteers at the shelter for women and children, he does the same work he used to be paid for.

Other times, Suelo has taken what most would consider a "real job." A friend in Moab owned a salmon boat in the Bering Sea, and in the spring was always recruiting deckhands for the summer season. "I've always wanted to go to the Aleutians since [I was] a kid," Suelo wrote. "What was holding me back was I didn't want to spoil my moneyless venture." In the summer of 2007 Suelo signed on under one condition: he wouldn't get paid. Captain Rayburn Pride paid Suelo's round-trip airfare, and off they went. The crew of three worked around the clock in the notoriously dangerous conditions of an Alaska trawler. On days off, while the others hit the bars, Suelo slept out in the woods, looking for bear and foxes.

When word got around Port Moller that this eccentric gray-haired dude who camped with the grizzlies was working *for no money*, something like outrage spread across the docks. The young bucks earning their living and their pride in the salmon fleet dubbed him "Free Bird."

The experience was eye-opening for a man who hadn't held a regular job in some time. "The hardest part of this has been living under such restriction, especially since I haven't had 'gainful' employment nor a boss for the past 7 years," Suelo wrote. "My life has been under the captain's authority 24/7—for this is how a boat must run. The first few weeks were really hard for me, like I had reverted to bumbling childhood & adolescence again."

After Suelo and the crew met their salmon quota a few weeks

early, the others decided to fly directly home. But Suelo wanted to hitch around and see the country. Captain Ray insisted on giving him five hundred dollars for his travels. (The other deckhand had earned ten thousand dollars for his season.) Suelo refused it, but Ray pressed, so Suelo solved the problem by hiding the cash on the boat as they locked it up for the season. The men flew to Anchorage, and when they parted ways in the airport, Suelo admitted what he had done. The captain was mildly annoyed, and pushed another two hundred into Suelo's pocket. Suelo followed the men as far as the gate and hugged them good-bye. Then he stepped outside, deposited the two hundred dollars in a bus shelter, and set off walking along the railroad tracks, living the next few weeks off wild peas, berries, dandelion greens, wild mushrooms, and salmon plucked from the streams with his bare hands.

Suelo's various volunteer labors should not, however, obscure his true vocation, which is something like freelance philosopher. He spends his days in conversation, with friends or with strangers, talking politics, economics, love, and God. He is a patient listener, and people who might otherwise lack an audience take full advantage of this trait. On the many days I ate with him at Free Meal, I had to check his forehead to see if there wasn't an invitation stamped there: PLEASE TELL ME YOUR CONSPIRACY THEORY.

Occasionally some dreamer who has heard about Suelo will arrive in Moab looking for enlightenment. Suelo will spend a few days with the pilgrim, share his food, play tour guide to the best dumpsters and the prime caves. One woman who took the bus from New Orleans had never slept outside or seen snow, did not like walking long distances, and was afraid of bicycles.

A more promising student, Roy Ramirez, was a twenty-four-year-old professional poker player from East Los Angeles, one of the few male members of his family to avoid the illegal drug trade and its inevitable incarceration. After a short stint in the military and a custody dispute with his ex-girlfriend, Roy began to seek a more spiritual, less materialistic life. One day he typed the words "living without money" into Google, and was directed to Suelo's site.

Roy bought a backpack and some outdoor clothing, and his parents delivered him to Moab, where he pledged to live an entire year without money. Roy didn't love the silence of the canyons, so with Suelo's guidance he squatted in an abandoned house. He was clean-cut, handsome, charming, and articulate, the kind of guy you'd put on a poster for achieving the American Dream. Roy became a regular at Free Meal, poised on one knee in the grass in his sleeveless shirt like the high school linebacker he once was. He set off for a moneyless adventure, hitching to New York and Washington, sleeping in truck stops and eating from dumpsters, proudly posting photos on his blog. His tutelage was earnest, if a bit remedial.

Roy: "The Bible doesn't say anything about Noah taking dinosaurs on the ark."

Daniel: "Oh, yeah! Of course, I tend to not look at it literally."

When Suelo is not talking, he's writing. When he was in his twenties, his goal was to "settle down (if that's possible for me) and work on my writing, which I consider to be my true career." By a circuitous route, he's achieved that. He has chronicled his entire adult life in Proustian detail: fifteen years of handwritten letters—thousands of pages—to family and friends, and another fifteen years of mass emails and online journals. He tried his hand at a few books over the years, but he burned the manuscripts before seeking publication. Some of his writing is plain great. If somewhere in the Smithsonian there is a collection titled *Americana: Hard Times, Poetic*, I nominate this letter for inclusion:

> *I went down to the train tracks and ran into a 60-something toothless hobo I'd met days before. He was nursing a beer and setting up camp at the underpass. "I was surprised when you came up and talked to me the other day. People usually don't talk to me," he said. I vented my cop woes onto him. He asked if I had a Bible. "Yeah, I found one in a dumpster," I said. "I like to read the Bible," he said. "Keeps me from getting lonely." He told me I could hop a train all the way to Bakersfield.*

. . .

THESE DAYS Suelo is a fixture at the Moab Public Library, where he maintains his blog and website, and responds to hundreds of emails from all around the world. For years, he sent group emails reporting his travels and musings, but then began posting on the blog instead. His website is a permanent information clearinghouse that outlines his philosophy. It includes quotes from Lame Deer and Abraham Lincoln and the Apostle Paul, a detailed set of Frequently Asked Questions ("You look well-dressed and well-fed; are you a trust-funder?"), and a library of Suelo's own essays, with esoteric titles like "The Seven-Headed Dragon: World Commerce" and "Contradiction Between

Eastern Religion and Christianity: Non-Dualism Embraces Dualism?" And thanks to public libraries, and free net services like Gmail, Blog*Spot, and Google Sites, Suelo has set up his cottage publishing industry without paying a cent.

Though he has published a few pieces in arcane journals, it goes without saying that Suelo does not get paid for his writing. But that's not uncommon in this line of work. And unlike many so-called legitimate authors, Suelo can boast of an audience. He garners a few thousand readers per month, and his blog posts usually draw a couple dozen comments. Having myself been paid to deliver fastidiously researched and revised articles to national magazines, only to have them hit the newsstands without a blip, I envy Suelo his passionate, if adversarial, readership.

Never one to shy from debate, Suelo cruises chat rooms and his own comment threads, responding to questions, clarifying, or just plain bickering. On a website called MatadorChange, people were discussing whether Suelo was a "social rebel or simply a mooch." A commenter named Jane came down on the side of mooch. "If you want to have something, then do your part to make sure others can have that thing too," wrote Jane. "If you eat an apple, then plant the seeds or water the tree. If you consume a resource, find a way to replace it or come up with an equivalent so that the person whose resource it was could replace it for you."

Suelo was sufficiently tweaked to reply. "Jane, it might do you good to study the Kung Bushmen of the Kalahari, before and after they got 'civilized.' You might also want to check out the FAQ on my website before you pass more judgment on me, somebody you have never met."

"I've passed no judgment on you," Jane snapped back. "You

take from others (discarded things yes, but you do still take them) without giving anything back in return."

Now Suelo lectured her like a condescending Socrates. "I know whether or not your statement is true, and you know that I know whether or not it is true, because it is about me. But do you know that your statement is true? This is what I mean by passing judgment."

The whole argument could have been avoided if Suelo had detailed all the ways he does, in fact, "give back." But Suelo would rather argue until blue in the face than defend himself in that way. During a year of interviews, I heard secondhand accounts of Suelo's volunteer work, but he never told me about it himself. He confirmed that he'd done the work, but never offered up the information without prodding. He prefers to say, "To those who assume I don't work. It may or may not be true! But why do you assume it? Must one toot one's own horn before work is valid? Must one work for one's own credit (money), publish it, before work exists?"

At first, I took his reticence on the subject as sheer stubbornness. It wasn't until I studied the Sermon on the Mount that I finally figured out his motivation. Most theological discussions with Suelo come back to this sermon, in which Jesus says:

Be careful not to do your "acts of righteousness" before men, to be seen by them. If you do, you will have no reward from your Father in heaven. So when you give to the needy, do not announce it with trumpets, as the hypocrites do in the synagogues and on the streets, to be honored by men. But when you give to the needy, do not let your left hand know what your right hand is doing, so that your giving may be in secret.

The same message is in the Tao Te Ching:

Creating without claiming,
Doing without taking credit,
Guiding without interfering,
This is Primal Virtue.

． ． ．

ON A WINDY spring day I caught up with Suelo at Sol Food
Farms, where he was volunteering. Although he often leaves
Moab for cooler climes in the summer, in 2010 he decided to
stick around to work on the farm. It was a cause he believed in.
And although he chose his own hours and didn't receive pay, it
was the closest thing to a regular job he had had since salmon
fishing three years before.

Sol Food's acres extended between a new tract of largish
homes and a wild thicket, in the same fertile creek bottom where
Suelo had been harvesting melons the previous fall. The owner,
Chris Conrad, began the enterprise in 2008 by leasing these
fields that, until recently, had grown food for generations.
Friendly and affable, with a toothy grin and wavy hair pouring
over a visor, Chris described a sense of mission larger than
merely growing tomatoes: he was also reviving a tradition of
local agriculture that dated back to pioneer days. He told me
that the name of his business stood for "Sustainable, Organic,
Local." "But legally I can't call it organic," he said drily. "The
government owns that word."

Chris and Suelo showed me around the farm. The carrots
planted in late fall had survived the winter and were bushy on

top. Chris pulled a few and we washed them beneath a spigot and chomped on the sweet orange roots. He showed me the hoop house—a twenty-by-thirty-foot homemade greenhouse with a wood frame, steel ribs, and sheets of clear plastic. The structure had prevented the ground beneath it from freezing during the recent winter—the coldest on record—but had then collapsed beneath the snow, requiring an expensive rebuild. Chris took evident pride in what he'd created here, the neat rows of spinach and Asian greens and turnips. "You can eat those turnips like apples," Suelo said. A six-foot fence encircled the precious crops and kept the deer at bay.

Like many permanent residents, Chris Conrad came to Moab for a seasonal job and ended up staying. After graduating from college in his native Pennsylvania, with a major in natural resource management and a minor in philosophy, he took a summer volunteer position at Dead Horse Point State Park, which morphed into a paid seasonal job. Over the years he worked as a guide, an ambulance driver, and then, feeling what he calls "societal pressure to get a real job," he worked four years as director of the county's emergency medical services. But then he decided he'd had enough of wearing a pager. "I'd read enough philosophy and financial freedom books—and had been lucky enough to live as a climbing bum—so that I knew there's a life to live." He quit his job and started his own photo business. In 2008 at the age of thirty-four he ran for a seat on the Grand County Council, and won. A year later he launched the farm.

The first year was tough. He hired some farmers with more experience than him, and they clashed. "Maybe I just didn't have the leadership skills," he told me. "I couldn't get them to do what

I wanted them to do." So in Year Two, Chris eliminated paid labor and was running the farm with volunteers who worked for vegetables.

The workers that day were Suelo, Brer Erschadi—the founder of the Moab Free Meal—and a kid who'd just graduated from Rutgers with a degree in psychology. He told me he had come out to Moab to "live," as opposed to "sitting in an office and going into debt, which is what it would take to pursue my career or go to graduate school."

I hadn't actually come to the farm intending to work, but when I asked Brer if he had a minute to talk, he handed me a rake and said, "Sure, can you help us with this?"

It was a beautiful day in the orchard. Suelo and Brer swung hoes into the shallow irrigation troughs that had clogged with grass and leaves over the years, and the rest of us hauled the downed branches and limbs across the field to a burn pile. The orchard was decades old, but as far as Chris Conrad knew, its pears had never been brought to market. He planned to do just that.

We piled the branches onto a plastic tarp and dragged it through the orchard rows. It had been a long winter where I live in Montana, and the desert sunshine was like honey. Blossoms hung from the trees. It felt good to use my hands and feet and muscles. What's more, we weren't just working, we were restoring this paradise to its glory. Whoever planted these trees had given up the dream, and we were keeping it alive. The sun melted the clouds, crisp April wind blew, and the five of us caught the euphoria that comes from hard outdoor labor. Instead of resenting the boss and counting the hours, we were here by choice. Conversation skipped along from the coming global water shortage to Vipassana meditation to the outrages perpetrated by the Federal Reserve Board. We pulled our rakes and swung our hoes with a consensus of purpose.

Suelo, in a pair of leather work boots, shorts, and a black T-shirt, was throwing a hoe. Beads of sweat dripped from his hat onto his forehead. Over the course of an hour he'd dug a long straight trench the entire length of the orchard, a segment of the old network of irrigation ditches cut by pioneers. He leaned on the wooden handle of the hoe and inspected his work. "The Taoists believe that the devil walks a straight line," said Suelo, "so they grow their crops in a zigzag."

And then, with the ditches clear, the moment arrived. Chris Conrad pulled a lever, and a stream of spring snowmelt bubbled from a plastic pipe. It filled the newly cut ditches, pouring down the gentle gradient, building mass until an apron of tiny brooks flooded the fruit trees, the soil soggy underfoot, our boot heels sinking in muck. We were bringing the desert to life. We were doing good work.

8

. . .

*Connecting Grand County with the outside world was not
an easy task.*

—Richard Firmage, *A History of Grand County*

IN THE SPRING of 1974, Conrad Sorenson fueled up his Volkswagen Beetle and set out for Santa Fe from his home in Salt Lake City. He was carrying five hundred dollars in cash, with which he hoped to pay down on a few acres in the desert. Like many in those years, he was fleeing the city for the land.

With his long hair and Bug, Conrad resembled a typical hippie. He worked at a health food store and oversaw its book inventory—titles about women's issues and American shamans and Eastern mysticism that in those days were hard to find in a mainstream bookstore. In 1968, he'd ridden his motorcycle to San Francisco, turned vegetarian, and spent the next few years flying back and forth to Salt Lake, occasionally packing kilos of grass in his leather trousers.

But unlike many back-to-the-landers, Conrad wasn't some kid surfing the latest trend. He was thirty-four years old, and had been born into a working-class Mormon family in Ogden.

His mother sent him to classical piano lessons, and to this day he can still resurrect the exquisite chaos of Schubert and Chopin on the baby grand his mother willed him.

After two restless years at Brigham Young University, Conrad shipped to Germany as a missionary for the Latter-Day Saints. The year was 1960, and the stirrings of the counterculture were still faint, but he already sensed that he didn't belong in a dark suit spreading the gospel. "I went on the mission to please my parents," Conrad says, fifty years later. "They knew full well I didn't believe a word of it."

Now in his seventies, Conrad Sorenson lives in a studio built against the side of a Moab cliff, with a wagon wheel as a window. The exposed red-rock wall and cast-iron woodstove and a shimmering brass gong give his home a Middle Earth feel, and Conrad, with his slight frame and delicate hands, graying ponytail, and scruffy mustache, fits the role of reclusive gnome. His hobbit hole has neither television nor telephone. He prepares his meals on a hot plate. The grand piano fills the room like a ship in a bottle.

"Suelo is like John the Baptist, the Essenes, continuing a tradition that has run through our history, and all cultures—a lineage," Sorenson told me, referring to the early bands of Jewish mystics. "He's like Basho, the old Japanese wanderer and monk who wants nothing, is trusting of the universe to deliver, and accepts what is delivered."

I went to see Conrad because he has known Suelo for twenty years, and as canyon country's godfather of pilgrims, in some ways he paved the way for Suelo. While pockets of freegans have sprouted up all across the country in the past decade, most are in cities—Portland, San Francisco, Buffalo—tolerant urban communities with plenty of waste to be scavenged. But for two decades Suelo has always returned to the most right-wing state in the nation. "I've always felt like Moab was unusually nonjudgmental," Suelo says. "Even conservative people here don't seem to care whether I'm homeless, or gay. Once in a while someone says something, but they seem the minority, whereas in most towns they are the majority."

Suelo's circuitous arrival in Moab resembles that of Conrad. After a year on his mission in Germany, Sorenson's supervisors sensed he was ready to bolt, so they offered him a plum assignment: playing piano in a traveling dance band called the Internationals. These minstrels would jazz up meeting halls with swing and standards as a way of attracting a younger crowd. "Then the guys in shirts and ties would pass out the Mormon lit."

Back in the States, Conrad dropped out of BYU and, in order to gain a draft deferment, enrolled at the University of Utah. He joined the premier campus choral group and fell in love with an alto who shared his passion for descending caves in the Wasatch Range and meandering the stone mazes of the canyon lands. But she was a dyed-in-the-wool Mormon, and it didn't work out. By the time of his road trip toward Santa Fe, he had abandoned the expectations of his upbringing. He had had affairs with both men and women, and was buying property with a German woman two decades his senior whom he met while singing hymns and playing the pump organ at a Mormon meeting in Germany. The five hundred dollars with which he was to purchase their piece of paradise actually belonged to Gerda.

En route to Santa Fe that glorious sunny day in 1974, Conrad stopped in Moab. He often passed through the bleak uranium town on his hiking getaways to Canyonlands National Park.

Conrad was a prodigious explorer, but not your typical Boy Scout with a rucksack laden with folding shovel and rain slicker and trail map and compass. He was an aesthete. He was less interested in reaching some destination—a river or overlook or arch—than in the *experience* of traveling through the moonscape, visualizing steps and ramps on a sheer slickrock dome, squeezing into forbidden slots and wondering if there was an exit. He sought to become an element of the landscape, just like the knotty juniper trunk or the bobbing lizard or the swirls in the sandstone. There were few places in the world as conducive to this sort of mind-altering tourism as southern Utah, and on almost every hike, after a few hours of rambling, Conrad could find some little nook or box canyon where, he was certain, no other human had set foot. That was a thrill that rivaled the melodies in music. To attain these epiphanies, Conrad employed some unorthodox outdoorsman's techniques. The first requirement was a few lungfuls from his personal West Coast stash. The second was to remove all his clothes.

His journeys had given him little reason to celebrate the dinky gateway towns that opened into his wonderland. He judged Moab in particular—with its dominant architectural style of single-wides, cinderblock tract houses, and Quonset huts riveted with sheets of corrugated metal—a godforsaken place. "I couldn't get through it fast enough," he says.

But this time he had a peculiar quest: to locate a cult author whose books on Gestalt therapy were available only through a tiny outfit called Real People Press, which was located, of all places, in Moab. Gestalt therapy was a midcentury intellectual phenomenon that combined elements of post-Nazi existentialism, Zen Buddhism, psychoanalysis, and experimental theater in the service of learning to experience life in the present moment. The author, a cantankerous British woman named Barry Stevens, was said to be an associate of such prehippie mind-blowers as Aldous Huxley and Bertrand Russell, and in the early seventies had emerged as an unwilling guru of the human potential movement, thanks to a series of books she'd produced, with such heady titles as *Don't Push the River (It Flows by Itself)* and *Person to Person: The Problem of Being Human*. Now, according to rumor, she had, in a Mr. Kurtz kind of way, gone native in the recesses of the desert.

Conrad found the street address and inquired after the author, only to be informed that Ms. Stevens lived in seclusion and did not accept visitors.

"She's not friendly," he was warned. "She might tell you to fuck off."

But Conrad persisted, and was given a set of labyrinthine directions. He set out along the Colorado River on a road that was only partially paved, winding through the black-streaked loaves of sandstone. After not too long, he came upon a sign advertising five-acre plots. He climbed a muddy spur road and emerged into a sublime paradise: sheer red-rock monuments thrust up from a green valley toward dazzling white alps. A mild breeze blew the sweet scent of fruit blossoms. Lazy cows munched on grasses. It was like some idyllic Swiss haven—only in the desert.

After thirty miles on the river road, seven miles on a rugged mining trail, and driving his Bug across a broken bridge, he arrived at the ranch and found his quarry to be an absolute sweetheart. "For some reason I had brought some mangoes," he says. "And it turned out she was a mango lover." The two talked like old friends, and she offered him a place to camp out for the night. Conrad gobbled a pot brownie and lay there under the explosion of stars, listening all night to the horrifying howls of beasts, which he thought might be a hallucination, but which Ms. Stevens informed him in the morning were coyotes.

Conrad never made it to Santa Fe. He spent the five hundred dollars as a deposit on a homestead, and he and Gerda settled, she in the dilapidated log cabin and he in a sod-roofed outbuilding tucked into a cave with a cottonwood trunk as its ceiling beam. They have lived there ever since.

A bisexual dope-smoking Jack Mormon who speaks fluent German and whose passions included spelunking, choir, motorcycles, nude hiking, feminist literature, and classical piano might be hard-pressed to assimilate into even the most tolerant of communities: in a hick Utah mining town he was a clear outlier. But in Moab, nobody blinked an eye; they never did. Indeed, when I told locals that I was writing a book about a guy in a cave, they asked, "Which one?"

Let's back up. The myth of the American frontier tells us that the West is the forge in which effete Easterners are hammered from soft boys into steely men. Been that way forever, or at least since 1804, when Lewis and Clark opened the frontier to the Pacific, entering as gentlemen in tailored coats and returning as woodsmen wrapped in buckskins. The mountain men who followed are legendary: Liver-Eating Johnson, Kit Carson, Jim Bridger, and Jedediah Smith. Theodore Roosevelt was transformed from a bespectacled Harvard geek to a swashbuckling Rough Rider by his hitch in the West. And something about the virgin forest inspired massive productivity—made men want to cut that lumber, build cabins and lodges and bridges, plow the fields, and carve a permanent place for their race. In the 1800s they felled swaths of timber to build such bustling cities as Denver and Seattle and Portland.

But the myth of the mountain man does not account for one critical fact about the West: most of it ain't mountains. It's desert. Huge swaths of California, and most of Utah, Colorado, Nevada, Arizona, and New Mexico, receive fewer than ten inches of rain per year. Instead of pine forests and aspen groves, they are dotted with gnarled piñons and junipers, knee-high brush and prickly cacti. Pioneers on the southern route found scarce timber to chop down, precious few streams to divert, and hardly any land fertile enough to yield a carrot. To this day, you can drive hours across the Southwest without finding a single shade tree.

During the nineteenth century, white Americans could find little use for the vast desert except as a place to lay railroad and dig mines—neither of which attracted the hearty ax-wielding types who gravitated to the Northwest. It wasn't until the twentieth-century swelling of the federal government, with its subsidized highways, dams, canals, and electrical lines (for air-conditioning, mostly) that the American desert was truly settled in places like Los Angeles, Phoenix, and Las Vegas. These grids of sprawling concrete attracted even fewer Paul Bunyans than the outposts they replaced.

In short, the desert draws a different type of person than the mountains, one whose place in American lore has been largely ignored because it doesn't fit the Manifest Destiny mythology of the industrious settler cutting a civilized swath in the savage forest.

When I first rolled into the desert at age twenty-two, it was more by accident than design. My attempt to move to the Rockies had failed, and when the road to my second-choice destination was closed, the hitchhikers I'd picked up suggested Moab. That sounded fine. I wasn't out looking for America, or for myself: I was trying to get away from both. Judging by the cluster of billboards and drive-thrus we encountered on Moab's main drag—even then, in 1993—I hadn't gone far enough. But eventually the remoteness of the place became clear. Grand County is the size of Delaware, yet contains fewer than ten thousand humans. When I moved there you had to drive more than an hour to see a movie or buy a pair of shoes. So I stayed, and soon fell in with others like me, and like Suelo, who'd abandoned professional ambitions to wait tables or collect rocks or build adobe houses, who were drawn here partly by the grandeur of the place, but more by the sanctuary it offered from the world outside, or by some dissatisfaction with the place they'd been before, or by just plain restlessness.

These, it turned out, were my people.

While the mountains have their Lewis and Clark and Theodore Roosevelt—mature, reasonable, moralistic—the icons of the desert are different: a mixed bag of dreamers, pilgrims, outcasts, and wanderers. Brigham Young brought his flock out here not to establish an American foothold, but to build a kingdom outside the country that had persecuted them. "The desert and the parched land will be glad," predicted the prophet Isaiah. "The wilderness will rejoice and blossom." (While no one could argue that the Mormons' vast empire around the Great Salt Lake is impermanent, its outposts in the southern canyon country, more than a century after their settling, remain that: outposts.) The land's native sons, Cochise, Geronimo, and the Mormon cowpoke Butch Cassidy, navigated the wilderness mazes as a fortress from the invasion of modernity. Georgia O'Keeffe and Frank Lloyd Wright were drawn to the other-worldly geometry and isolation, and former park ranger Ed Abbey's hymns like *Desert Solitaire* almost single-handedly transformed the perception of the place from a wasteland best left to dirt bikes and miners to a mecca of untamed wonder. And then there is the California teenager Everett Ruess, perhaps the desert's most enduring saint. Ruess wandered the desert alone in the 1930s, seeking art and inspiration, declared to his diary, "I have seen almost more beauty than I can bear," then sank into Glen Canyon and was never seen again.

Which is not to say there have been no achievers in canyon country. Padres Dominguez and Escalante set out in 1776 to find a route from Santa Fe to California. The prospector Charlie Steen made a fortune when he struck uranium, and built himself a cliff-side mansion that he christened Mi Vida after the mine that helped usher in the era of American atomic power. But for all its discoveries, the Dominguez expedition eventually failed, and looped back to New Mexico. And Steen lost his millions on high living and bad investments; his trophy home, long since sold, is now a steak house called Sunset Grill, with a row of flags out front and a sign proclaiming TOUR BUSES WELCOME! Each spring a new crop of gift shops and eateries in towns like Moab cut their grand-opening ribbons, and each winter an equal number close up shop for good.

We don't come to the desert seeking the square-jawed ranger and rustic old lodge that invoke the settling of the frontier. We come because the desert feels not yet settled, like another country—or another planet. Its hardscrabble shacks and trailers are as puny as the price sticker on a painting. The scenery is too large to comprehend. It clobbers us. And instead of being inspired to make some permanent mark on the landscape, we sense the permanence of the landscape itself, and the fleeting nature of all human endeavor. In the desert we see the eternal. So while the mountains became a proving ground for manhood, the deserts remain the proving ground for the spirit.

It's no surprise, really. Historically, deserts are where religions are born. "I will send my messenger ahead of you, who will prepare your way," says the prophet Isaiah: "A voice of one calling in the desert." That voice is understood to be John the Baptist, who lived alone in the desert, eating locusts and wild honey. It was during Jesus's forty days in the desert that he faced off with the devil and resisted the temptation of a human existence. The holy cities of Mecca, Jerusalem, Bethlehem, and Bodh Gaya are all in the deserts. One might argue that this is only a historical coincidence, the result of Jesus, Buddha, and Mohammed being born in the desert. To which I say: what if Jesus had been born on the Oregon coast? You can bet he would have started chopping down trees and building cabins to get out of the rain—and history would have been very different.

· · ·

THREE ELEMENTS MAKE Moab singularly attractive to those looking to get lost. First is its geographical isolation and wildness: "The country was almost inaccessible and it was a bold sheriff who would follow the sandrock trail in search of his man," wrote historian John Riis. "So Moab became the *rendezvous* for gunmen and robbers." Butch Cassidy's Robbers Roost was nearby, and his notorious Wild Bunch would now and then ride out of the canyons and shoot up town. One of them even killed the sheriff. (This sort of thing continues. On November 19, 2010, a man shot a ranger just outside of town, fled into the canyons, evaded a posse of 130 officers, and hasn't been seen since. When Moabites studied the comparable topography of Afghanistan where U.S. forces were for so long hunting Osama bin Laden, they shook their heads and concluded, "They'll *never* find him.") The isolated residents apparently preferred it that way. In 1897—the same year builders broke ground on that icon of modernity, the Eiffel Tower—Moab still had no road or railway service, and the only way to cross the Colorado River into town was by ferry. Boosters added to the ballot a ten-thousand-dollar bond to build forty miles of road to the railroad depot. Voters swatted it down by a tally of 74–6. A graded road and river bridge did not arrive until 1912.

Second, Moab has always had a reflexively antiauthority bent. People came here to do whatever the hell they wanted. When in 1878 a settler named Arthur Barney crossed the Colorado where Moab now sits, he and his men found a sign on the bank reading NO CAMPING ALLOWED. In excellent Moab form, they threw the sign in the river and crossed. Half a mile later they met a homesteader woman and asked her about the prohibition on camping. "This is a free country and you can camp where you please," she said. When Barney mentioned the sign, the woman snapped, "You ought to have throwed that notice in the river."

The third and final defining element of Moab was a certain, not to say "sloth," but people here were just *different*. They worked as hard as it took to survive, but not a lick more. They didn't have that drive that made frontiersmen famous. As early as 1900 a local doctor diagnosed Moab Fever. "Its chief symptom was laziness, and it was prevalent locally because it was so easy to survive in Moab but so difficult to get wealthy there," reports historian Richard Firmage. In modern times, that ailment has been renamed the Moab Eddy, after the river feature in which water circles indefinitely without venturing downstream. It has caused many a young man and woman to squander a college education working low-status, low-stress, and low-paying jobs such as waiting tables, monitoring campgrounds, or rowing boats.

As a result, Moab attracts plenty of hermits, and it's natural to list Suelo in their ranks. But a hermit is someone whose mistrust of humanity is so complete that he chooses isolation. The hermit will barter for sustenance, but considers the process a necessary evil, the weak link in his quest for total independence. Suelo's rationale for giving up money is the opposite. "In America we have this idea that everyone should be self-sufficient, pull yourself up by your own bootstraps," Suelo says. "A lot of people think that's why I'm doing this. But really it's about acknowledging that there's not a creature or even a particle in the universe that's self-sufficient. We're all dependent on everybody else. I'm dependent on the hard work of other people, just like they're dependent on mine. But to say we're all dependent on the money system is a different thing."

Quitting money has not impeded his ability to join a community. Quite the opposite—Suelo is a social butterfly. When he and a friend, a Buddhist monk, were camped in Marin County, California, they would pore over concert listings in the city weekly, then pedal their clunkers across the Golden Gate. Parking their bikes (unlocked, of course) at the box office for a Ravi Shankar show, the monk explained to the bouncers that he and Suelo lived without money, and would like to see the show. The doormen whisked them on through. When in Portland, Suelo is a regular cook and participant at the Food Not Bombs free meal served in a city park. The month he squatted on the University of Florida campus proved a cultural smorgasbord. "I've gone to free films, some talks, Quaker services, Krishna feeds and events, Jewish events, a Muslim event," he wrote. "I even got to hear a talk by Elie Wiesel, Holocaust survivor & Nobel-laureate author. I also get free personal concerts from guys who come out to the forest boardwalk to drum, as well as a righteous bluegrass banjo player who comes out to pick for fun. I've made nice friends here."

And while he's home, his social calendar is packed. He's been known to play poker, losing the buy-in floated by a friend. "He's a fabulous dancer," reports Melony Gilles. When a good band is playing at the bar, she offers to pay his cover charge. I've attended music night in Conrad Sorenson's lair, with Chris Conrad and Brer Erschadi blowing didgeridoos, Suelo banging a gong, and Sorenson lying on his back under the piano, howling into the reverberating strings. For Suelo's fiftieth birthday, he invited friends on Facebook to a potluck at the home of Damian Nash. BYOB, naturally.

The Moab community that embraces Suelo did not hatch overnight. And the reason I return to Conrad Sorenson is that the health food store he operated there for two decades was the hub of the town's bohemian subculture, a beacon toward the moneyless life that Suelo has since adopted.

By the time Sorenson arrived in 1974, the quiet farm town had emerged as the uranium capital of the world. In 1956, *McCall's* magazine reported that, as home to between twenty and thirty millionaires, Moab had the world's highest concentration of them. The most notorious, Charlie Steen, liked to charter his airplane to circle above the valley so he could watch television—the town was still too isolated to pick up broadcast signals. The uranium frenzy brought booming business in the mills and mines, and workers flooded in from out of state. Local kids dropped out of high school to earn twenty dollars an hour and buy their first house. And with the establishment of Canyonlands and Arches national parks, in 1964 and 1971 respectively, the town became a seasonal magnet for visitors, and a year-round residence for rangers and administrators. This influx of tourists, rangers, and miners gave Moab further diversity, and even tolerance.

Conrad and Gerda launched Moab's first health food store, which, in addition to the spelt and quinoa, served her home-baked pies and distributed his eclectic taste in literature. The store closed after four years, but by then hippies had gained the critical mass to form a cooperative, purchasing bulk oats and polenta and selling them to members from a small storefront three days a week. Conrad volunteered to manage the floor, and after some disagreements with the directors, dissolved the board and took the helm. As a result, although Conrad was able to sign checks and access the bank account, he was never legal proprietor. "It was an unowned business," he says. For almost two decades, the Moab Co-op was a case study in utopian anarchy, with Conrad as the benevolent dictator. Nobody—including Conrad—was ever paid a wage. Volunteers recorded their hours in a ledger and were then allowed to take approximately four dollars' worth of food per hour. The system was loose. "I never looked at the book," Conrad remembers. "We got ripped off regularly. But something was working.

"My mission was to provide organic food at cost," he says. Any profits were either poured back into the business or outright given away. Living rent-free in his sod hut, Conrad could afford to give away hundreds of books and loads of food. He particularly prided himself on sussing out a stranger in a few short minutes, and then gifting an appropriate book. Among the browsers at his first store was noted author and philanderer Ed Abbey. "I had a sexy woman behind the counter," Conrad says. "He came in to chat up the boobs." Conrad gave him a book about feminism.

"By giving things away right and left, by having no interest in turning a profit, we had loyal customers from Salt Lake City and Colorado who came to shop," he says. "They saved so much on food that it paid for the price of the drive—and they got a little vacation. I put thousands of dollars into the library. Despite all that, we grew twenty percent each year."

The co-op ultimately rented an entire building—an old plumbing shop constructed of World War II wooden ammo boxes with a canopy of trumpet vine shading the porch. More than half the building was dedicated not to retail, but to community space. There was a free lending library with thousands of titles, an art and dance studio, a xylophone gallery. On the back sofas you might find women nursing babies, couples making out, somebody waking up after crashing there for the night. Conrad lingered nearby—he says he worked about eighty hours a week—offering free advice on herbal remedies and love affairs. Below the surface of Moab's Mormon ranching and mining establishment lay a counterculture, and the co-op became its den, Conrad its Fagin.

It was through these doors that Daniel Suelo walked in the winter of 1992. Damian Nash had invited his friend to come live with him while he recovered from depression. On the evening of Suelo's arrival, Nash was screening movies in the back room. Suelo found the old building. The wooden door creaked and as he crossed the concrete slab floor the place smelled of tamari and lavender oil. In the aisles, men in cutoffs and flip-flops stocked the shelves with hand-packed baggies of granola and dried mangoes. Behind the counter, a dreadlocked girl in flowing skirts, baby on hip, weighed out grains on a stainless-steel scale and punched the numbers into an antique register.

"People who live this lifestyle ended up at the co-op," says Suelo. "And of course that planted ideas in my head. Showed me that there were alternative ways to live." Moab provided the community that Daniel had sought. Soon he began working the floor in exchange for food, one of his first steps toward forsaking money.

Beyond the co-op, Suelo found other sectors of the Moab community where the value of money wasn't a given. He landed a job as a prep cook in a health food café. "It feels really good doing mindless work," he wrote to a friend. "And the people I work with are great people. So many folks in Moab are so down-to-earth. It's refreshing." Chopping spinach and boiling beans in Honest Ozzie's felt more like hanging out in the family kitchen than going to work. "It really feels nice getting my concentration off 'career' and onto life," he wrote. He felt "more and more a part of humanity, with no hierarchy—not separate from, not above or below anybody—just a common member of humanity. Loving our neighbor as ourself! That is what life is all about."

This was where I met Daniel in the summer of 1993, on my own nebulous quest to pursue life instead of career, and I can attest that Honest Ozzie's was a good place to do it. Ozzie's was situated in a converted old cottage with plenty of outdoor seating, and it specialized in natural foods like locally grown pinto beans, whole-wheat pancakes, and all things soy-derived. Having worked a summer flipping burgers, I was hired on the spot as breakfast cook—the previous guy had quit to float the Grand Canyon. (Nobody asked for my résumé, with its bachelor's degree in English literature.) With waiters and cooks like me more interested in living than working, Ozzie's was the kind of place where forty-five minutes after the waitress took your order for veggie enchiladas, you might get up to investigate and find her doing cartwheels on the lawn with a golden retriever.

But the food was great and who cared about the customers, right? It was a fine time to be footloose in Moab. By then the Atlas uranium mill was boarded up, and in that brief window between the uranium and mountain-biking booms, one could live virtually for free in the most spectacular place on the planet. Jobs were plentiful and easy to get—in cafés and bike shops and white-water raft outfits. Wages were strictly minimum, but rent was negligible. Mere river guides were buying cinderblock homes for no money down, just picking up the hundred-dollar mortgage payment after the miners packed up and left.

And once it got hot, who needed a house anyway? A few newly met friends and I circled our dented station wagons in a thicket by the creek and lived in our tents all summer. All our needs were met. We bathed in the river. Food was easy enough to come by—guiding and restaurant jobs fed us on the clock— and the co-op was dirt cheap, or even free if you volunteered. Each night during happy hour at the Rio Bar and Grill we drank dollar pints and ate half-price nachos and chicken fingers—a fine meal for less than five bucks.

Suelo did not simply decide one day that he'd live in a cave. Just as giving up money was an incremental journey over many years, giving up a home was something he did gradually. In the same way that men who are obsessed with prostitutes become vice cops, Suelo's fascination with the homeless had led him to work in shelters, and while he'd been working in Denver, something happened that changed his perception of charity. He'd been invited to sit on a panel on homelessness for a sociology course at CU. The students invited a handful of social workers and a handful of residents of local shelters. To spice things up, they also trawled the Boulder Mall and brought back a smattering of punks and hobos panhandling on the streets. All three groups sat onstage together.

Daniel and his colleagues spoke first, and painted a grim picture. They blamed Reaganomics and unconstitutional city ordinances and plain greed and callousness in the human heart. "Woe is the world," is how Suelo recalls his talk. He offered as the solution: more people like us, more funding, more institutions. In short, *we* are needed to help the poor. And then the poor themselves spoke up, and were equally morbid. Woe is the world times two! They railed against unjust economic practices and a playing field that was anything but level, and had nothing but gratitude for the selfless caseworkers like Daniel who helped them in their time of need. Consensus had been achieved.

But wait: the street people spoke up.

"I don't see what's so bad about living outside," said one. "It's a big party, if you ask me."

"Yeah, fuck the shelters," said another. "Life is free!"

Suelo mulled this over in Moab. Why was he so terrified of being homeless? Was it the physical hardship? No. He loved camping and being outdoors. He thought that pitching a tent in a windstorm and figuring out how to stay dry through the thundershowers was fun. No, the real fear of being homeless lay in worrying what other people would think. The stigma. And he thought: *If I can overcome what people think about me, I can overcome anything.*

In Moab, homelessness was not only acceptable, it was sort of romantic. Everyone was doing it: itinerant rock climbers and river guides and cocktail waitresses. Instead of a stigma, home-lessness had cachet—a reverse status symbol! Suelo had arrived, finally, in a town where money was the filthy lucre of creeps—and living without a home was cool.

When his second spring in the desert bloomed, in 1994, Suelo was staying at a friend's house, and had been asked to house-sit in the summer. But for the coming months, he had no home, and the rental market was tight as the seasonal workers flooded back. He gathered his backpack and his courage, along with a stray mutt he'd found on the river, and wandered up a nearby canyon. Suelo poked his head into a musty cave. He took a step, then waited while his eyes adjusted to the half-light. He unrolled his pad and sleeping bag. He trembled with exhilara-tion. If only for a short time, he had joined the ranks of the homeless.

The same month, he landed a job as the homeless coordina-tor at the women's shelter, thus earning the ironic nickname of "Homeless Homeless Coordinator."

"I got such a kick out of it," he says. "It gave me an edge with the clients."

As the summer heat arrived, vagabond men would land at the shelter—which only housed women—and ask to be put up in a hotel. Suelo explained that the budget was small, and they were conserving it for winter. "We have vast public lands all around us," he counseled them. "And the weather is beautiful."

"That's easy for you to say," the men grumbled.

"Yeah, it is," said Suelo. "I'm camping out."

Suelo liked the work. Absent was the hierarchy and hypoc-risy he'd felt working with the homeless in Colorado. In Moab the line between haves and have-nots was not as distinct. Suelo had found his niche—a good job that didn't require moral compromise, a community that accepted him, and a way of living homelessly without shame.

"The desert reminds me that there is sanity in existence," he wrote to a friend. "This place is just so beautiful. It's morning and the sun is just starting to shine through the canyon walls and sparkle through the leaves of the cottonwoods below me. The breeze is cool and I have my dog by my side. Ah—life is good."

9

. . .

My lover thrust his hand through the latch-opening; my
    heart began to pound for him.
I arose to open for my lover, and my hands dripped with
    myrrh,
my fingers with flowing myrrh, on the handles of the lock.
I opened for my lover, but my lover had left; he was gone.

—Song of Songs

SUELO ARRIVED IN Moab still a member of the Celibate Club. His romantic life till then had crashed in waves of self-pity. Looking back at what he called the midlife crisis of his thirtieth birthday, he wrote: "I had never been in any kind of relationship and was feeling withered and without hope and chronically lonely."

On that first night watching movies in the back of the co-op, Daniel was introduced to a gentle lion named Rocky who was into hiking and literary theory and had recently been excommunicated from the Mormon Church. He was strong and fit and freckled, with a mane of strawberry hair. Damian had met Rocky at a Quaker meeting and thought the two would be a good match. Like Daniel's, Rocky's coming-out had been a cataclysmic rejection of his upbringing. His LDS childhood rivaled

Daniel's fundamentalist roots in intensity. The two hit it off—just as Damian had planned—and Daniel's first romance blossomed. "Rocky and I could walk around holding hands, and people don't seem to care," Suelo says now.

The acceptance he found in Moab, however, was not equaled within his family. In the four years since coming out, Daniel had insisted to his parents that being gay was natural. The Shellabargers had done their best to put his sexuality into biblical perspective. Their conclusion: like Daniel the prophet, their son was a eunuch, an idea that Daniel himself had floated before coming out. They clung to a belief that Daniel's lack of appetite for women was brought on by the loss of one testicle during college, after a case of testicular torsion—a belief for which there is no scientific basis. His family believed that his longing for other men was a sin, but as long as he didn't act upon it, it was not a mortal sin.

"I was trying to maintain a relationship with my family and have no religion," says Suelo. "I labeled myself an atheist. I felt like I needed to build some bridge with my family. And it's impossible to do that as an atheist."

Daniel's coming-out was just one in a series of trials that befell the family. Around the time Daniel went to college, Dick Shellabarger had left his job at the dealership and was hired as a minister in a newly formed evangelical church. With all five children grown and out of the house, the couple settled into the parsonage, seeing a stable and pleasant future for themselves. But hard times were just around the corner. In 1987, while Daniel was in the Peace Corps, his sister, Pennie, left her husband and brought her eight children to live at the rectory. Within the year, Dick's father died, Daniel wrote his coming-out letter from Ecuador, the minister job fell apart, and the family was forced to

move. Sixty years old, Dick and Laurel had no means of supporting themselves, much less their eight grandkids. The Shellabargers took a job as relief managers for Motel 6, traveling from state
to state for short stints wherever they were needed. They lived
briefly in Wyoming, New Mexico, Montana, and Nevada, then
finally landed a permanent position in Salt Lake City—which
is where they got the news of Daniel's suicide attempt. Eighteen
months later, just as Daniel was settling in Moab, came his
brother Rick's diagnosis with the brain tumor; he was dead
within a year. After an onslaught of such Job-like proportions,
the Shellabargers were inclined to suspend their most severe
judgment when Daniel brought Rocky to visit them at the Motel
6 in Salt Lake City, and they welcomed the "friend," relieved that
their youngest son, though perhaps not what they had hoped
he'd be, was at least alive and healthy.

For Daniel, the liberating thrill of romance soon gave way to
the messy business of an actual relationship. Rocky saw fireworks
and wanted a lover. Daniel wasn't so sure. Maybe he was just
lonely. He wanted space. He rented his own apartment. "Things
are starting to get a bit more realistic between Rocky and me,
and we're finally starting to develop a friendship like we shoulda
done from the beginning," he wrote to Tim Frederick. His pur-
suer persisted. "I can't get space from Rocky," Daniel complained.
"I consider him one of my best friends (but not a lover)."

Real or not, the affair with Rocky plodded into the next year.
The romance ended when Rocky dropped by unannounced and
accused Daniel of acting irrationally. "He wouldn't leave when
I told him to, so I physically pushed him out the door and shut
it," Daniel wrote, just minutes after the fight. "I've never done
anything like that to anybody in my life. Working at the women's

shelter and learning about abusive disorders has given me a new empowerment and I feel good."

As he is prone to do in the face of disappointment, Suelo waxed philosophical. "I am actually feeling kind of privileged being a late bloomer. Guess I feel better being a cherry tree than a tulip. And I still haven't been in a real relationship."

Though still depressed, Daniel was entering his first stable period in a decade. He worked part-time at the shelter, and took other odd jobs—pulling espressos, substitute teaching, grading exams for a local company that taught English to Japanese students via overnight mail. He and Damian Nash pooled their meager funds, along with some cash from Nash's mother, and for five thousand dollars purchased a dilapidated trailer home, stripped to the studs by the meth heads who had inhabited it. Damian and Daniel hauled the thing to a ramshackle trailer park at the mouth of a canyon and began renovating. Daniel paid a nominal rent of one hundred dollars per month that Damian banked as Daniel's share of partial ownership.

In the meantime, Daniel pressed on in a quest for Real Love that would sweep him into a state of ecstasy he'd so far found only in prayer and male friendship. It hitchhiked into town the following summer.

One day from the trailer Daniel saw a young man walk past on his way to the canyon. He had a limp and no backpack or sleeping bag—just a Mexican blanket and a conga drum slung over his shoulder. His hair was dark and curly and his skin olive, and he had a world-weariness about him, an old soul. He was elfin and mysterious, like some feral creature raised by coyotes. Daniel was transfixed—not just by the boy's beauty, but by his lack of possessions. How could someone live like that? Daniel sensed immediately that he and this youth were destined to meet.

It happened a few weeks later. Daniel was reading poems at an open mike in a coffee shop—some pretty esoteric stuff, the result of his chronic malaise combined with his lifelong fascination with biblical numerology.

The Seven Heads are Seven Mountains
On which the Woman sits
The Tower of Babel
has touched
heaven

The stranger approached afterward. He loved the poems, he said. He spoke in a bizarre sort of cockney, the result of having spent part of his childhood in New Zealand. The more he spoke, the more exotic and alluring he became, like some pirate spawn from a Robert Louis Stevenson novel. He'd sailed around the world with his father. The reason he limped was that as a child he'd had polio. He was only nineteen but had already lived an eternity. He had this aura about him. Everyone in the room was drawn to him. Especially Daniel.

Daniel invited him up to the trailer. They lit a few candles and uncorked a bottle of wine and talked until late. Daniel had never felt such a connection. Mathew ended up sleeping on the couch. Daniel lay in his own bed, his heart thumping, the dawn wrens beginning to sing.

The two became inseparable. Mathew spent nights in the trailer, and they camped out in the canyon, tucked into caves and alcoves or just lying on the rock beneath the stars. But when Daniel revealed that he was gay, Mathew said that he was not. Daniel couldn't believe it. The energy between them was too strong.

Then one night, Daniel felt Mathew's hand creep over his shoulder and slide across his chest. A bolt shot along his spine. Hardly able to control his breathing, he inched his hand toward Mathew's until they touched. Mathew recoiled.

This happened night after night. It was driving Daniel crazy. He confided in Conrad Sorenson at the co-op. "Be patient," Conrad assured him. "You two belong together." The pursuit continued. Some nights Mathew would hold Daniel for a few minutes, then leap out of bed, returning an hour later and dozing off.

Finally Daniel's persistence paid off. One night, as he remembers it, the walls fell down. They fell into each other's arms and confessed to be madly in love. Total bliss. As winter approached, Mathew moved into the trailer, and the new couple became happily domestic.

"Mathew is plastering over the fake wood-grain paneling and rounding the corners in the bay-window room," Suelo wrote. "We're then going to paint a rain forest on the walls. It's starting to look less and less like a trailer in here."

Like most new lovebirds, the two appeared unutterably adorable to each other, and nauseatingly self-absorbed to everyone else. "Sometimes I'd hear Mathew and Daniel giggling and flirting in the bathtub through the paper-thin walls, candles lit," remembers Damian Nash. "I'd have to go outside and take a walk. They were both unbelievable slobs. You had to wade knee-deep through the junk not put away."

It was an eccentric household. Damian, a nationally competitive chess player, was a psychology teacher who would eventually coach Grand County High School's chess team to become state champions. (Later he would take a Colorado team to its respective championship as well, and in 2010 he became Utah State Chess Champion.) He held a master's degree in neuroscience and cognitive science and was a practicing Quaker, but self-identified as a "mystic groupie" with a personal set of beliefs derived from Rumi and the Sufi poets. His girlfriend, Linda Whitham, was a fetching New Englander with a master's degree and a Protestant work ethic; she clocked at least forty hours a week for an environmental group, and had never caught or understood the Moab Fever that induced such loafing.

Such eclecticism was not the exception but the rule in the Powerhouse Lane Trailer Court. Nestled beside a peach orchard and a clear creek on a rutted dirt road at the mouth of the canyon, the run-down collection of Airstreams and Detroiters had gained the nickname "Third World Trailer Park," largely for the pack of stub-legged mutts that ran wild at all hours, menacing passersby with their howls and supplying the city shelter with ample broods of stub-legged pups. The property had been all but abandoned after the uranium mill closed in 1984, with just a few holdouts hunkering beneath the mulberry trees. But when a local hippie bought it and planted apples and peaches, and began renting berths for sixty-eight dollars a month, the place quickly filled up with manufactured homes well past their prime. The new owner, Andrew Riley, had only two rules: no meth, no pit bulls. "If they showed up and had a deposit and rent, I let them in," Andrew says. He is now in his sixties, with white hair and a face burned pink by years in the orchard. "I usually had a waiting list to get in."

And what sort of people chose to dwell there? "Quality people who didn't want the responsibility of ownership" is how Riley characterizes them. But as someone who twice took up residence in the

Third World Trailer Park myself, I'd say my neighbors shared a certain je ne sais quoi which in these parts could be called "Moab Chic." I'm talking about people who rip through a tin wall with a Sawzall to build a straw-bale adobe addition, who thatch privacy fences from hand-harvested willow shoots, who sink wood-fired hot tubs into their driveways. Among the forty or so inhabitants were a navy veteran, a Broadway dancer, a New York fashion model, the hobbled author of the definitive guidebooks to rock climbing in the Canyonlands, the ethereal publisher of a Jungian journal called *Dream Network* ("Evolving a Dream Cherishing Culture"), as well as the usual muster of river guides, seasonal waiters, Indians, environmental activists, and drunks. The only non-wheeled structure on the lane was a collapsing cottage leased as a crash pad for Outward Bound guides, whose fleet of dented pickups and campers were overgrown with green tumbleweeds during the August monsoon. Surnames were seldom spoken, and denizens went by Hippie Bruce and Wild Man Jimmy, Rattlesnake Kate and Stormin' Norman. What the place lacked in the pit bulls and meth labs that typify so many trailer parks, it more than made up for in love triangles (and quadrangles, and pentagons), bitter feuds about stupid shit, and fires ignited by smoking in bed.

"There is strange energy on that property," Riley says. "Something dark had happened there, maybe with the Indians." Indeed, the trailers were parked a short jaunt downstream from panels of Anasazi rock drawings that give some people the heebie-jeebies. Over the years, Wiley employed increasingly unorthodox methods of healing the land's bad juju, including one ceremony with the dancing and drumming of "witch women." ("Where did you get the witches?" I asked, scribbling notes. He looked away and murmured, "Just have to know where to look, I guess.")

On a night that, for my money, typifies the glory days of Powerhouse Lane (the court has since been dismantled), Damian brought home the Russian chess master Igor Ivanov to sleep on the couch. Ivanov was in town for a tournament Damian had organized, and he wanted to save hotel costs. The four men—Daniel, Mathew, Damian, Igor—opened a bottle of vodka and argued politics all night. (Linda was presumably out of town or had the good sense to knock off early.) The Russian was six foot seven and about three hundred pounds, an ultraconservative who had defected from the Soviet Union. With each shot of vodka, he bellowed louder that communism was the world's greatest evil, how it squashed creativity and eradicated the individual. Tiny Mathew, the leftist elf, would not be bullied. He stood toe-to-toe with the ogre, matching vodka shots and railing point for point about the abuses of fascism and corporations.

At dawn, as Damian drove the sodden Russian to the tournament, Igor said with begrudging respect, "He's a young man with much to learn. But at least he defends his ideas." He was so hungover that he lost the match.

The reverie between Daniel and Mathew bubbled through the winter, eventually straining the relationship between Damian and Linda. One night Daniel and Mathew left a candle lit and accidentally burned a hole in Linda's beautiful rug, a gift from Damian's mother. They tried to conceal the burn beneath a piece of furniture, but it was discovered. Daniel did not apologize to Linda, and she took her case to Damian. She was tired of having to share her home and her life with this freeloading, insolent, chronically depressed mooch and his demon lover. She gave Damian the ultimatum: him or me.

Three days later, Linda moved out.

Soon the drafty trailer carried too much responsibility for the happy couple, and as spring blossomed, Daniel bought an old Chevy van for five hundred dollars. They planned to split the summer between the van and the canyon. But even as Daniel followed Mathew into reckless freedom, he chafed at his lover's unpredictability. Daniel wrote, "Sometimes I think Mathew is an old-soul sage mature way beyond his years, sometimes (maybe more often than not) I think he's a 7-year-old trapped in the body of a 20-yr-old. It makes me glad I'm going on 35."

Daniel was jealous of Mathew's friendship with a woman in the trailer park who liked to joke that Daniel was Mathew's sugar daddy. When quizzed about her, Mathew grew defiant. A triangle formed. Mathew spent more and more time with the woman. "Mathew was exploring, Daniel was settling," says Damian. Finally, Daniel couldn't stand it any longer.

"Are you in love with her?" he demanded.

Mathew started laughing. "Why in the world would you say that?"

"Well, aren't you in love with the person you spend the most time with?"

Mathew didn't answer.

So Daniel stormed over to her trailer and asked her the same thing. She laughed, too. It was demeaning. He was furious.

The next day Mathew was downright cavalier.

"I've been thinking about what you said," he said. "I think I am in love with her. You opened my eyes."

And just like that, Mathew and the neighbor packed up her car and left for parts unknown. Love blew out of town as easily as it had blown in.

"It's been utterly devastating," Daniel wrote to Tim Wojtusik, his closest friend from the Peace Corps. "Just when I think I've explored all the byways of pain, I find there's a new, even more intense one to relish. I feel so incredibly betrayed. My heart's been broken and shredded and used to wipe Mathew's ass. So strange that I didn't realize how very much I love him— the pain is overwhelming."

At work, the English exams from Japan gazed up nonsensically from his desk. Four days later, he quit. He slept in his van and had little contact with friends. But even as the pain sharpened, he noticed something peculiar: It was real. It wasn't the sort of metaphysical ennui that had depressed him for five years. This pain was different—more visceral and human. He wrote, "Deep down I knew all this shit would happen and I needed to go through it for some sick reason."

The current misery of heartbreak was preferable to the previous miseries of loneliness and existential angst. He wallowed in it. He spent two months in the canyon, lingering in the sites where love had sparked. "It forced me to face things," he wrote. "All kinds of shit surfaced and I did a lot of crying, as well as laughing and feeling joy and beauty."

Suelo emerged believing that maybe he just wasn't cut out for relationships. "I keep thinking that if I can feel 100% comfortable with being alone, then I'll know how to do this human-interaction thing," he wrote. "I often feel foolish for having put so much importance on my little vapor-in-the-wind relationship. I've had so little experience with romance that the rare times it has happened I haven't known what to do with it, like an adolescent."

In terms of Suelo's journey, the loss of his relationship with Mathew represented the loosening of one more worldly attachment. In mythological terms, we might call the romance his meeting with the Temptress, one of the many trials the hero must overcome. It was also the last significant romance of his life.

"I'd be completely happy if I never had a relationship again," Suelo says today. "And I'd be happy if one came. But it's not something I'm going to go looking for."

In the fifteen years since his heartbreak, Suelo has had a few flings, but nothing that lasted more than a couple of months. He mused after one such failed affair, "My lifestyle is a bit much for him."

Suelo's closest friends see his love life as problematic. "I think not being in a relationship is his great suffering," Damian Nash says. "He was happiest when he first came to Moab, because he was young and the prospect of love was very real. Back then he was falling in love with the land, having the best sex of his life. Now he's given up on that, resigned himself to the solitary life of a monk."

"He was at that time more consumed with finding a lover," says Conrad Sorenson. "He has become much more of a monk."

And yet he hasn't entirely given up on love. When I was in Moab interviewing Suelo, a strikingly good-looking kid hitched into town. Cody was wiry and androgynous, with blond dreadlocks, an ox ring in his nose, tattoos rising out of his collar. He was in his early twenties, and after reading Suelo's website had come to find him. The two camped out together, talked late into the night about God and love and the cosmos. Cody kept referring to his "ex-partner, Jesse." The stage was set for tragicomic misunderstanding. The whole thing unfolded in Suelo's excruciating candor on his blog.

"I told Cody he can now tell everybody that he came all the way to Moab and caused me to fall crazy in love with him. Just when I'd thought I was immune to all that. Totally unexpected . . .

He's got a beautiful girlfriend [Jesse] back in Colorado he is madly and faithfully in love with, and he is young enough to be my son. In other words, I'm trying to pick up my heart weighed down by crushing, unrequited, romantic love."

I had to admit that I didn't think this fifty-year-old man in a cave was being realistic about his romantic options, especially when chasing straight guys half his age. One night after dinner at my trailer I asked him: really, what kind of man, even if he is gay, is going to move into a cave and stop using money, just for love?

"It's almost like I set myself up to make it difficult," he conceded. "Setting up the field of natural selection: if they can make it through, they're the one I want. That's part of our mythology, our fairy tale. The feminine and the masculine. The feminine— the princess—sets up obstacles. The masculine has to go through these twelve trials, conquer the dragon, or whatever. It's like biology. The egg is sitting there, and the sperm have to go through this toxic fluid to get to it."

I asked why he didn't spend more time in a city with an actual gay population.

"I was turned off by the gay community in Denver," he told me. "It was too easy." He paused. "People weren't refined."

Refined? I was floored. To me, "refined" meant piano jazz, pinot gris, knowing which fork is for salad. "You live in a cave," I said. "How can you complain that other men aren't refined?"

"My idea of refinement is someone who can stand on their own, without all these fluffy comforts. When I think of refinement, I think of ore refined through the fire, all the excess is burned off. Just the gold."

It's a gloriously—you might say impossibly—romantic ideal. It made me wonder if Suelo really wanted to find someone, or just to pine away for the unattainable. Maybe he was like Snow White, or Moneyless Beauty, putting himself through ridiculous hardship with the secret hope that Prince Charming might one day kiss him back to life.

"How much of your life is just a reaction to not falling in love?" I asked. "Do you think you were driven into solitude by a broken heart?"

"Yeah, I think that had a lot to do with it," he said. "Mathew . . . I felt it was an enlightening experience. There was a turning point there, where I felt like: why should I put so much investment into things that aren't lasting, that are temporary, like relationships? But I've had people ask me over the years: isn't this just an excuse? A compensation for not having a fulfilling relationship? Maybe it is. I feel like every single thing we do in life is a compensation for something else. This is just the path I've chosen, and it's the most fulfilling. I felt like a relationship would spoil that, unless it was a relationship where somebody was willing to do this with me. But it's put me in a spot where it's very unlikely, too. So does it mean I'm afraid of a relationship, that I'm running? Maybe."

10

. . .

Take courage, boy! The Earth is all that lasts.

—Black Elk

ALONE IN THE canyon one April day in 1997, three years before quitting money, Suelo attempted to eat a live animal. "I got hungry and caught a sand lizard," he wrote. "He went totally limp, fully giving himself to me. I put his body in my mouth and bit his head off."

This is one of my favorite moments in all of Suelo's writing, because it obliterates my occasional suspicion that he is merely on some practical quest for survival. No, this is a man looking to solve life's mysteries. In the preceding months he had come up with a theory about food, the spiritual bond between the eater and the eaten: "Cultures the world over consider their staple the incarnation of God: Buffalo for the Cheyenne, Corn for the Hopi, Cattle for the Massai, Wheat (bread) for the Christians. What I've seen about hunting and gathering peoples, they are the only ones who can fully grasp and accept the Holy Communion. (Funny how we think we have to cram our little wafers down their throats.) All life forms are the sacrificial victim—there's absolutely no exception; all are food."

Like any good scientist, Daniel endeavored to test his hypothesis—with alarming results. "I tried to swallow him but spit him out in revulsion," he wrote. "The root of all life, and I'm revolted!"

It was no coincidence that Daniel was conducting this experiment on Passover—the feast thought to have been the occasion for Jesus's Last Supper. On the verge of crucifixion, he instructed his disciples that bread was his body and wine his blood, and that they should partake in remembrance of him. So you see: Suelo wasn't eating this lizard for protein. For that he would have cooked the thing. Rather, he wanted to understand *spiritually* what it meant to consume another life. To be granted life through the death of another. You might call it training for the day when some other creature—whether a grizzly bear or an earthworm—consumes him.

Daniel's Passover Seder concluded: "So I thought, 'This is my body,' and tried again. I swallowed him, tasting the pungent blood. After that, everything in the canyon smelled like lizard blood—even my own sweat."

The Last Lizard was a particularly memorable episode in Suelo's attempts to test the philosophical framework for the moneyless life, in the years leading up to his decision. In a broad sense, he was trying out two theories about the good life. The first came to him courtesy of Henry David Thoreau. As a million pairs of soon-to-be-chapped lips have recited at the head of the Appalachian Trail, "I went to the woods because I wished to live deliberately, to front only the essential facts of life, and see if I could not learn what it had to teach, and not, when I came to die, discover that I had not lived."

But before Suelo could begin to discover what the effects might be of living simply, free of artificial distractions and closer to the rhythms of nature, he had to prepare himself even to embark on such an experiment. He had arrived in Moab pickled to the gills—like 10 percent of Americans in the 1990s—on a skull-warping cocktail of Prozac, Zoloft, and Wellbutrin. When one antidepressant stopped working, they'd give him another, and when a few replacements crapped out, they'd revert to the first. The problem with Zoloft was that it made his mouth dry and his brain fuzzy. Once, while being interviewed for the local television station about a Habitat for Humanity program he was launching, he got so parched that he started to stutter right there on camera. Then it seemed to him that the buzzing of the neon light overhead grew deafening. Worse, when he looked up at it, he discovered that there was no neon light—the buzzing was inside his skull. "Luckily no one watches that station anyway," he says.

One day, blinking into the sun as he stepped out of the post office, he bumped into his former roommate, Linda Whitham. She asked how he was and he couldn't fake it.

"Shitty," he said. "I'm out of a job. Anxiety attacks. Life sucks."

She looked at him with supremely kind eyes.

"Don't worry about anything," she said. "Not jobs or money. Until you find your health. That's what's most important. Concentrate on that."

A little light switched on—not the buzzing neon in his head, but a pleasant bulb illuminating some forgotten corner of will. He resolved that day to cure himself of depression without the use of pharmaceuticals. He began splitting the pills in halves, then quarters, then eighths, then finally he flushed the last of the particles down the toilet. His naturopath friend Michael Friedman suggested a natural alternative, St John's wort, which Suelo began brewing as tea three times a day.

"I started visualizing my thoughts," Suelo says. "My mind was a weed garden of negative thoughts about people, things, myself. I thought: 'I don't care if it takes me until I'm eighty years old—I'm going to weed out this garden. That's my priority.' I kept seeing these negative thoughts rising in my mind. Why do I hold on to them? It's useless. I'd let it go."

And slowly, living in his cave through 1997, his mental health improved. He would look up from what he was doing and notice that he hadn't been unhappy in hours. The depression had begun to evaporate. Thrilled by the progress of his mind, he began to focus on his body.

Even on an emotionally good day, physically Suelo still felt bad. His stomach fought most of what he fed it—the chronic gas and indigestion was so bad that he wondered if he was carrying a parasite from his stint in the Peace Corps. He was dizzy and his head ached. And mostly he was just plain tired—so tired he didn't want to get up in the morning.

Dr. Friedman diagnosed chronic fatigue syndrome, and prescribed antifungals and digestive enzymes. They seemed to help, enough that, for the first time in a decade of feeling feeble and sickly, Suelo dared to imagine himself strong and robust. As the youngest in his large family, Suelo had lived his whole life as the weakest and the littlest, the one who could be bossed or scolded or pushed around. No more. Having expended so much energy protecting his right to differ from the norm of masculinity—to be sensitive and feminine without apology—suddenly he realized he didn't have to choose. He could have it both ways. Hell, he wanted to be a man!

He began putting his body to the test. When he finished his four-day shift as a live-in assistant at the women's shelter, he'd spend the rest of the week alone, deep in the canyon, farther up than he'd ever camped before, a full two-hour walk from town. He didn't see anyone up there, and the long walk filled his calves with blood and his lungs with cold air. He stayed the entire winter in a north-facing alcove where the sun rarely hit, and the trickling spring froze solid. He got a second sleeping bag and didn't allow himself a campfire—he wanted to see what he was made of. He adopted a strict diet: organic, vegan, raw. His body weathered the winter with just the protein of nuts. "I feel like I'm in my prime," he wrote. Suelo's stint of simplicity in the wilderness appeared to reveal, as Thoreau promised, that man thrives in nature.

The second theory that Suelo was exploring had to do with chance and fate. From his observations of the natural world, he suspected that free will is mere human myth, and that the time we spend planning and worrying about the future is folly. While there are a few industrious exceptions, like beaver and squirrels, most wild animals don't plan ahead. They take what is available—that is, plants and bodies of other animals—and when they die they give what they have: their own bodies.

Suelo found support for his theory in Jesus Christ Himself. After years of cutting himself off from the religion of his parents, he was giving it another look. In the Sermon on the Mount, Jesus articulates the core principles of what was to become

Christianity: love your enemy, turn the other cheek, judge not lest you be judged, the meek shall inherit the earth. And he also talks about nature.

"Look at the birds of the air; they do not sow or reap or store away in the barns, and yet your heavenly Father feeds them. Are you not much more valuable than they?" In other words, if God provides for the birds, wouldn't He also provide for humans? And then Jesus gets into the revolutionary stuff—things that weren't stressed in Suelo's upbringing: "Do not worry about your life, what you will eat or drink; or about your body, what you will wear. Is not life more important than food, and the body more important than clothes?" And then the kicker: "Who of you by worrying can add a single hour to his life?"

It was a breakthrough. Suelo's anxiety had been the cause of so much misery. He was always worried about what would happen next, where he'd live, how he'd pay off his student loans, what his parents would think. And now here was Jesus Himself saying that worrying won't get you anything, won't add an extra hour of life, or as the King James has it, won't add a single cubit to your stature.

If the best-laid plans were folly, then did it follow that mere chance was divine? This was Suelo's hypothesis: "Chance is God. To know the mind of Chance you must break all attachments (preplanning) and move with chance. Faith = taking a chance." The corollary to relinquishing control of the future was assuming that whatever happens, happens for a reason.

Take Saint Francis of Assisi, perhaps the second most influential Christian after Jesus, who founded the Franciscan order of monks in thirteenth-century Italy and is credited with bringing vows of poverty to the religion. Il Poverello, the Little Poor Man, was one of Christianity's great renunciates, inspired by Jesus's famous teaching: "If you wish to be perfect, go sell all you have, and give to the poor, and come, follow me." His clothes were so shabby that, according to his biography, *The Little Flowers of Saint Francis,* "for a long time he had been going around Assisi looking contemptible and so mortified by penance that many people thought he was simple-minded, and he was laughed at as a lunatic and driven away with many insults and stones and mud by his relatives and by strangers."

Francis was a devout believer in Divine Chance. One day he and a fellow monk, Brother Masseo, came upon a crossroad with trails leading to Siena, Florence, and Arezzo. They didn't know which way to go. "We will take the road God wants us to take," Francis announced. Masseo wondered how they would discern God's will. Francis had it all figured out. "Now under the merit of holy obedience," Francis intoned, "I command you to twirl around in this crossroad, right where you are standing, just as children do, and not to stop turning until I tell you."

Masseo did as he was told, spinning till dizzy, stumbling and getting back up. Finally Francis called "Stand still! Don't move! What direction are you facing?"

"Siena?" Masseo said, gasping for breath.

"That is the road God wants us to take," said Francis. And off they went.

Juggling his two theories—Thoreau's premise that living in nature made you stronger, and St. Francis's belief that following chance brought you closer to God—Suelo soon had the opportunity to test them both.

. . .

As HIS SOLITARY spring of 1997 turned to summer, Suelo met two artists at a local gallery. San Francisco native Leslie Howes was thirty-one and had worked odd jobs in Moab for half a decade, including her own stint grading English papers from Japan. Having graduated from Exeter and Berkeley, and possessing real talent as a writer, painter, and actor, Leslie was a sterling example of the polished flotsam that circles the Moab Eddy. Pedigree notwithstanding, Leslie worked as a river guide and waitress and dated guys named Larry who drove motorboats for a living. Among the traits that endeared her to Daniel was a rapid fluttering of her eyelashes when she was angry, and a propensity to snort while laughing.

The other new friend was Mel Scully, a twenty-seven-year-old painter from Michigan who'd drifted into Moab for spring break, read a few Ed Abbey books, visited the co-op, hiked into the canyons, and called it home. "The middle of nowhere is fabulous," she told a friend. "It's the best place to be." She stayed for a while in a travel trailer outside the youth hostel, with an extension cord that snaked through the window to a bare lightbulb. There was no running water, but in exchange for chores she stayed free and could use the hostel's toilet and shower. Soon enough, she moved into a run-down A-frame with four vegans who forbade the cooking of meat on the premises. "Meat eaters are killing Gaia," explained the woman who owned the pots and pans. "Eventually, I felt too guilty to even open a can of tuna, so I became a vegetarian," Scully says, "but more out of fear and guilt than some profound insight into not eating meat."

When the two women met Suelo, there was magic between the three of them. Suelo was reading the Bhagavad Gita, Scully was reading Star Hawk, and Leslie was reading Virginia Woolf—somehow it all clicked. "My first human connection in eons!" he reported. Leslie told them about Alaska, where she had waited tables at a lodge the previous summer. She had photos: staggering mountains and green rivers and soaring bald eagles. It was a high-paying respite from the sweltering Moab doldrums. She was leaving in two weeks to go back. "If you bring black pants and black shoes, you can get a job in Denali," Leslie promised. "They'll give you a shirt."

"I'm in," said Scully, bound to neither her vegan slum nor her waitress job. They turned to Suelo. "Come with us!" they implored.

Suelo was enjoying his life in the canyon, and working hard to pay off his student loans. But then he started to think. Alaska! Wasn't that the real place to test his mettle in Mother Nature? And what about Chance? Hadn't he met these two women *for a reason*? Why be so attached to his plans? Why not go where the wind blew him?

The next day he gave notice at the shelter. And off they went.

"These are a couple of good women I'm motoring with," Daniel soon reported in a postcard. Yet things were a little more complicated than they first appeared.

It was true that Leslie wanted to return to her old job at the Princess Lodge, where senior citizens were deposited by train from the cruise ships for a glimpse of Denali and an evening of surf 'n turf and light opera. But it was also true that she'd fallen for an actor there, a member of the troupe that reenacted the 1913 first ascent of Mount McKinley. He was a strong-jawed, strapping fellow whose portrayal of expedition leader Harry

Karstens included at least one singing tap-dance number: "Don't let your feet freeze/Don't let your feet freeze/Gotta get gotta get—*to the top!*" While there may have been more significant obstacles to her romantic union with Harry Karstens, the most daunting by far was the three thousand miles of highway between the Canyonlands and Denali. It didn't help that Leslie was a notoriously poor driver, having wrecked a pair of vehicles in one-car accidents. "I partly invited Daniel to Alaska because I thought he would be a good driver," she admits fifteen years later. "He's very handy."

Mel Scully was also in love, and the object of her desire would prove even less attainable than the tap-dancing Harry Karstens. She had fallen, at first sight, hopelessly, madly, head over heels in love with the positively homosexual Daniel Shellabarger. And it wasn't until twenty-four hours before their departure, as the threesome cruised a supermarket parking lot in the Golden Egg—the nom de guerre of Leslie's Dodge van—that Daniel mentioned his ex-boyfriend and Scully realized that she'd made a grave error. "I turned bright red," she remembers. She hid her face. But anchors had been pulled. There was no turning back.

"Did you think maybe you could change his mind?" I asked her.

"I guess I did," she said. "I was young and naive."

The fact that the bond between Suelo and Scully was platonic did not curb their mutual infatuation. "You snore like a cute little kitten," Daniel cooed after their first night of camping. Leslie slept alone on the narrow top bunk of the van while Scully and Suelo shared the lower deck. At a hot spring in British Columbia, the chaste lovebirds floated on their backs and passed a cigarette back and forth, blowing smoke toward the cosmos. Leslie couldn't decide if she was jealous or plain nauseated.

"Which way do I turn?" Leslie would ask at a highway junction.

"Star Hawk says that East is Air, South is Fire, West is Water, and North is Earth," said Scully.

"Chance is our God," Suelo added.

Finally, when her shift was done, Leslie lay on her bunk with a pillow over her head as Suelo and Scully blabbed their heads off on the endless ALCAN Highway. Their point of most joyous consensus was that, yes, Everything Happens for a Reason. All sacred knowledge from Christ to Krishna, from the Wicca to the Spiral Dance, confirmed this. As did their encounters along the highway. Pounding over the potholes at dawn, they felt a lurch as part of the van's undercarriage thunked to the road: they'd broken a leaf spring. Leslie panicked. They pulled into a diner and at just that moment some Canadian fellow came along and took a look. "I can fix that," he said. And he spent the next two hours on his back under the van with his wrenches until it was good as new. They tried to pay him but he wouldn't accept a cent.

"You see!" said Suelo. "When we needed him, he appeared!"

"That was no coincidence," said Scully.

The next day, after snoozing through another spirited round-table on the generosity of the universe, Leslie poked her head into the cockpit to join a conversation about birth order. Suelo and Scully had discovered that they were respectively the youngest and middle children in their families, while Leslie was the oldest in hers.

"Younger children start revolutions," Suelo said.

"True. It's never the oldest," said Scully.

Leslie checked the map to find that they were forty miles from the nearest town, then examined the dashboard.

"We're out of gas," she observed.

They came across a tiny dirt road leading into thick woods.

"Maybe there are some people down there!" Suelo predicted.

Or maybe not. But they didn't really have a choice. They turned off the highway and coasted in neutral down the slight grade into deeper and deeper forest. It was nine o'clock at night and darkness was falling. Had they run out of gas for a reason?

"I think things happen for a reason if you have something to do with it," Leslie says. "For instance, if you are too stressed you might get a chronic disease. They both believe if you run out of gas in the middle of nowhere, there will be someone at the bottom of the hill baking cookies. I don't."

How wrong she was. Because as the Golden Egg sputtered to a stop at the bottom of the grade, they perceived the outline of a ranch house. A lumberjack of a guy emerged, and when they told him their dilemma, he pulled a red gasoline can from his shed and filled them up.

"Mother's pulling a batch of cookies from the oven," he said. "Come in and have a few."

· · ·

THEIR FIRST ALASKA destination was Homer, a fishing village on the Kenai Peninsula. Leslie vaguely knew a couple of people who lived there. That the men were gay was evidence enough that the town was some sort of bohemia. When I looked at a map, I saw that Homer was a full two days' detour from Denali.

"Wasn't that a bit out of the way?" I asked her.

"Was Paris out of the way?" she said.

By the time the Golden Egg rolled into Homer, the fractures in the trio's pilgrim spirit had cracked wide open. Suelo and Scully were keen to stay in a funky farmhouse where you could bale hay for room and board, a regular Alaskan kibbutz, a manifestation of the pie-in-the-sky they had been incanting for three thousand miles. Leslie took one look and thought otherwise: "It was a godforsaken youth hostel where everyone stole from each other." She departed in the van in search of Harry Karstens, and left Suelo and Scully on their own.

The budding best friends stayed together for a few more weeks. Suelo got the idea to work on a salmon trawler and tried to persuade Scully to join him. But by now, the hopelessness of her cause was apparent. "That's when I realized I didn't want to work on a fishing boat with the gay guy I was in love with." So they parted ways, with Scully finding a job in a lodge and Suelo alone in Homer, contemplating his options. "Money's almost gone," he wrote to Tim Wojtusik. "But I kinda get a kick out of flirting with chance."

He still wanted to test his theory, that if you stopped worrying and lived like the birds in the sky, the universe would provide. But he was afraid. "Well, Timo, I gave in to the stupidity," he wrote. "I put my ideals on hold, lost courage—and now I'm selling my self and my dignity to Snug Harbor Seafoods in the vile town of Kenai."

Suelo was slinging salmon from the tanks of ships into the big brailers that dumped them at the cannery. It was bottom-of-the-barrel manual labor—dirty, smelly, and wet—with low pay and no benefits and cramped living quarters, on call twenty-four hours a day.

Like most of the crew, Suelo bitched about conditions: "We work our asses off for little pay, with little sleep and little dignity—and I'm starting to realize how bad this is for my soul. I get into the work itself, in a Zen sorta way, but being under the authority of some pricks, just because they own more than I, whittles away at my spiritual health."

What differentiated Suelo from his fellow fish-slingers, though, was how he spent his free time: "I keep studying the Bhagavad Gita, the Tao Te Ching, the Sermon on the Mount, and the Gnostic Gospel of Thomas, and I've been reading bits and pieces of and about Henry David Thoreau, Gandhi, and Tolstoy, and I've written pages and pages in my journal, outlining what I'm supposedly learning."

He labored on for a month, hating himself for his compromises, confirming that this sort of worry was not adding a single cubit to his stature. Then one day the motorboat broke down. The boss had no choice but to charter as a replacement the skiff of his teenage son, and Suelo found himself taking orders from a thirteen-year-old. In the middle of a shift, he threw down his apron and walked off.

He hitchhiked across the peninsula to Seward, more determined than ever to put his hypothesis about Nature and Chance to the test. "I've thought about every single bit of work I've done for money, or even for barter-trade, that I've done in my life," he wrote to Wojtusik, sitting out the rain in an old church converted to a coffeehouse. "And I can't help but see and feel deeply that it is all wrong—totally wrong . . . The way out is still foggy to me, but now I feel it in my bones. I just have to step into the fog—either that or die."

And with that, he hiked into the Resurrection Mountains. "Seek first the kingdom of God, all these things will be added to you." Millions of people quote that bit of Scripture, but how many really try to prove it out? He had saved a few hundred dollars from his last paycheck, but intent on testing Providence, he didn't bother stocking up on food. In fact, at the trailhead he determined he had packed too much food, and deposited half of it on a picnic table. He knew the human body could survive a few weeks without food. "Look at the birds of the air," said Jesus. "They neither sow nor reap nor gather into barns, and yet your heavenly Father feeds them." He hoisted his soggy pack and marched into the woods.

The evergreens dripped with rainwater. The path wound through tufts of wet grass and thick alder brush. Moose pellets and bear scat dotted the trail. Dense fog seeped between the trees, and on the occasions when it lifted in the breeze, he could see jagged glacial mountains cutting into the sky.

And, yes, the Lord provided. Along the trail Suelo found plump berries bursting on the vine. He gorged himself. "I learned some amazing things eating raspberries in the woods," he wrote. "I mean these raspberries teach earth-shattering principles. We just don't see the simple truths (the power of Nature) when we get our food from the Supermarket." He feasted on blueberries, too. Low-lying orange berries with crunchy seeds were particularly nutritious.

Suelo strung his tarp between two trees by a lake and quickly finished his reserves of store-bought food. He had no fuel or stove. In the pouring rain, it took only a few days for doubts to creep in. "I started to think I was crazy," he says. "I was embarrassed." Chatting with other backpackers—the ones sautéing gourmet meals on their ultralight stoves—he did not mention that he was deliberately starving himself to test the message of the Sermon on the Mount.

This is really stupid, he thought. He was hungry. He couldn't stand the thought of another berry. His mind wandered to his college anthropology courses. Humans aren't supposed to live alone, he remembered. We're social creatures. Anthropologists have compared us to animal societies. Humans are in some ways closer to wolves than they are to apes. Biologically we rely on social interactions. Take the hunt as just one example—working together to bring down an animal. That's how the wolves coalesced as a pack. Suelo could see spawning salmon literally bubbling as they squirmed up the stream into the lake. Of course he had brought no rod or tackle. He tried halfheartedly to stab them with a stick but had no luck. He remembered reading somewhere about how the Inuit made pronged spears for catching fish. He looked dumbly at his pocketknife. *What I as a social creature really need,* he determined, *is for some Inuit to come along and teach me to spear fish.*

As he wallowed in self-pity, a young guy who had set up camp not far away sauntered up. *"¿Hablas español?"*

"Sí," said Suelo reflexively, then reflected on the coincidence: a dozen miles from pavement, three thousand miles from a Latin country, and the first guy to talk to him spoke the one foreign language he knew?

The man smiled and continued in Spanish. "I'm out here trying to live off the land. And I want to learn to spearfish. Do you want to come spearfish with me?"

Suelo leaped up. His doubts evaporated. The experiment resumed! Things were unequivocally Happening For A Reason.

The two men sharpened their sticks and began stabbing at the thick flow of salmon. After some trial and error, they lashed their pocketknives to the points of the spears, and before long they were hauling fish to camp and roasting them over a fire. The meat wasn't great—the salmon had gone to spawn and their flesh was past prime—but it provided protein the men craved. They sat contentedly beside the fire.

Ander was a twenty-year-old Basque from the Andalusian mountains in Spain. Like Suelo, he'd traveled to Alaska with some raw ideas about testing himself against the land. The two got to talking about Nature and Chance. Ander dug it. They decided to travel together. Between them they had no groceries, save a bottle of cooking oil that Ander had brought, which proved handy for panfrying salmon when they got tired of roasting them over an open fire. With their newfound spearfishing talent, Ander's expertise at foraging for wild mushrooms, and Suelo's familiarity with berries, they ate well.

And they could not escape the sense that some unseen hand was guiding them. One night as they finished another dinner of salmon and mushrooms, they got to talking about the foods they missed. Ander yearned for paella and Christmas dinner, but said what he missed most of all was coffee: dark roasted Colombian, steeped in a glass press and blended with cream. Suelo praised Thanksgiving turkey and stuffing and gravy. And s'mores.

Ander didn't know what a s'more was.

"You know, you roast a, how do you call it, marshmallow, on the campfire, press it between two graham crackers with a square of chocolate—"

"What is this—marshmallow?"

"It's white, fluffy, chewy," said Suelo. "Made of puffed sugar."

"I do not know this thing."

Suelo went on at length trying to explain a marshmallow. But it proved indescribable.

"Someday I'll show you one," he said. "Then you'll understand."

The men left their dishes by the lake as the rain poured. In the morning when Suelo went to wash them, he noticed a paper grocery sack. It was dry, meaning it hadn't been left out all night. He was curious. He peeked inside and saw what looked like groceries. That was awfully strange. Had Ander been holding out all this time? He decided not to let it bother him. Back under his tarp, he watched Ander walk to the shore to retrieve his plates. Ander did the same thing: peeked into the bag, then flashed a dirty look Suelo's way. All morning the men were standoffish. After all this talk about subsistence, one of them had apparently been hiding an entire sack of food in his pack. Finally Ander crawled out from under his tarp and said, "What's with this bag?"

"I thought it was yours."

"Well, I thought it was yours."

They crept up on the bag to investigate. They looked around. The other campers had packed up and left at first light. They were the only ones left.

Ander reached into the bag and retrieved something. A bag of chocolate-covered espresso beans.

They looked at each other, shocked. They pulled out the rest of the contents. Sealed packages of exotic Indian food, Madras lentils and Punjab eggplant and spinach paneer. A jar of Thai curry paste and a can of coconut milk. And what was this spongy thing at the bottom? Suelo pulled it hesitantly.

A bag of marshmallows.

HAVING STRIPPED LIFE to its essentials, Suelo felt stronger, sharper, more resourceful than ever. Relinquishing control to Chance, he saw that the universe was providing. Or was it?

Suelo and Ander hiked out of the Resurrections and hitched toward Matanuska Glacier State Park, encountering staggering generosity along the way—people who not only gave them rides but took them into their homes for the night, cooked a hot meal. At the last outpost, they purchased a few basic provisions and then camped at the mouth of the glacier. The blue water poured from beneath the ice into a swift, frigid river. And then things started to go bad.

"Let's cross the river and camp on the other side," Suelo said.

The river was too deep and fast to wade across. As they explored upstream, they found that in the transition zone between glacier and river, shallow water poured over a series of ice ledges. The men had no crampons or climbing gear, nor any experience on glaciers, but they decided they could cross. They waded across a cold channel and climbed onto the slick glacier, their toes instantly numb as their boots filled with ice water. The glacier was smooth and undulating, with a series of rivulets and pools where the runoff swept across. They took long steps over the cold channels. But then they reached a wider rivulet. The crystal water was so clear that Suelo couldn't tell how deep it was. Maybe two feet. Maybe six? The only choice was to jump. Suelo gathered his courage and with a few baby steps leaped across the gap, splatting on the ice on the other side but sliding chest-deep into the freezing pool. The cold water knocked the wind from his lungs. His clothes and backpack were soaked, adding another fifteen pounds to the load, and he clawed his way up and out onto the ice. Now Ander made the same jump, and was submerged over his head into the basin before Suelo pulled him out. Surging with adrenaline and panic, the men darted across the ice field, both dunking a few more times, before scrambling up the banks to dry ground—wet, shivering, and scared.

They built a fire to warm themselves and dry their clothes, but as soon as the flames flickered, the clouds darkened and rain began to fall. Suelo didn't see any chance of getting dry. They were too cold to cross the river back to where they started. He and Ander squatted over the fire as the raindrops spat on the branches. Both men understood that if they didn't do something soon, they could freeze to death.

"I'll go look around for shelter," Ander said. He trudged into the woods while Suelo wrung out his wool sweater and held it over the flame. After a while Ander returned.

"I found a cabin!" he called. "And it's open!"

The men packed their wet gear and jogged through the underbrush. Sure enough: a hunter's cabin was tucked in the woods. Inside were stacks of split fir and a cast-iron stove. Still shivering, they balled up bits of paper and kindling and stuffed in a few logs. Before long, they were warming their hands over a roaring fire as the rain pounded on the roof.

The storm lasted three days. Suelo and Ander strung their soaked sleeping bags and wool pants from the rafters as they fed wood to the fire. It was sobering to realize that they would not have survived in the cold rain with their wet gear. They ate all their provisions, not bothering to forage or fish in the pouring rain. On the fourth morning, the rain eased up and a hint of dull sunlight emerged. They heard the unmistakable buzzing of a Cessna overhead. It circled closer and closer. Were they being rescued? The men bolted out the door and waved. The plane was so low they could hear the hollering of the pilot. It sounded like cursing. And as the plane lifted a wing they heard it distinctly.

"Get the fuck out of there!" yelled the pilot. "Yeah, you! Get your ass out of my cabin!"

Then the pilot buzzed even lower and thrust some dark object out the window.

"He's got a gun!" said Suelo.

The men scurried back in the cabin, slammed the door, and hit the floor. Suelo felt his chest pounding. The buzzing of the Cessna and the tirade continued for a while, but at last the plane lifted and quiet returned.

Their clothes were dry and the rain had ceased, so Suelo and Ander packed up. Finding pen and paper, Suelo wrote a long note of thanks to whoever owned the place, apologizing for trespassing but noting that the misdemeanor had saved their lives. The men shouldered their packs and hurried back to the river, hoping to cut their losses and get back to safety.

Sheets of summer rain had swept across the glacier for days now, melting tons of ancient ice, and the river had swollen seven feet. The clear swift channel was now a frothing torrent, gray and cloudy as it churned up silt. It had not only deepened but widened to nearly a quarter mile. Swimming was out of the question.

The men explored the bank until they found a cable stretched across the river. On the distant shore was a rowboat tethered to a cable. But they had no way to retrieve it. Nonetheless, the cable glimmering in the sun above the white water looked more promising than the river.

Suelo clasped his hands over the steel, and with his pack straining against his shoulders, hooked his heels and inched his way along the cable. Ander followed. But after twenty feet, Suelo realized this was a terrible idea. The cold braids of steel dug into his palms, and the pain was unbearable. It took all his effort just to keep his grip. And then with a desperate yelp, Ander slipped off the cable, and the rebounding snap pried open Suelo's fist. In a jumble of arms and legs, both men plunged into the rapids. Suelo held his breath as the icy water pulled him below, then popped up for a breath and swam back toward shore. Luckily they weren't far. Both men crawled up the bank a hundred feet downstream from where they'd started. Ander was inconsolable.

"Eso es," he coughed, beginning to weep. "Our lives are over."

Suelo was thirty-seven and Ander was twenty. For the first time in his life, Daniel felt his paternal instinct kick in.

"We're going to be fine," he lied. "It's all part of the adventure."

"I don't want to die," wailed the Basque.

"No matter what happens, it's fun," Suelo insisted.

Their chances of crossing the river alive were about fifty-fifty. If they both went for it, they might both die. But if Suelo went alone and died, at least then Ander would have Plan B. Whatever that was.

"Stay here and don't worry," Suelo said. "I'll go get help."

Luckily it was warm and sunny. He peeled off his wet clothes and emptied his pack. He discarded all cotton garments that would only soak up water and keep him cold. He dressed head to toe in wool: socks beneath his boots, pants, a sweater, a knit cap and gloves. Then he hiked upstream to where they had crossed four days before. He would stick to that strategy— crossing where water rushed between fins of ice. He waded across the first channel and climbed the glacier. This time he encountered between ice fins not rivulets that could be leaped across, but deep, swirling trenches that had to be swum.

Here goes, he thought, and plunged into chest-deep water, dog-paddled for his life, then dug his fingers into the ice and belly-flopped onto the slab. That wasn't so bad. But the next swim was worse. The bathtubs gave way to swimming pools. Each time he clawed up the ice, he was sure he must be approaching the far bank, but each time when he stood for a view, the river seemed wider than ever. In the biggest pool yet, he groped up the ice, but it was too steep and slippery. He slid back in. The swirls held him under and he burst to the surface gasping for air. His backpack, filled with water, pulled him back below.

Your pack or your life, he thought. And in an instant he slipped his shoulders from the straps and let the current take the pack. Free of the load, Suelo scratched his way onto the ice and lay there panting. Surely he must be almost across. But he wasn't. He was less than halfway, perched on a block of ice in the middle of the river.

Gasping there on his knees, Suelo dropped his head to the ice and began bawling. The show of confidence he'd made for Ander was gone. He was cold and shivering and scared. Upstream, the glacier appeared as a living beast—a dragon—opening its jaws to consume him. He was going to die here.

But then something occurred to him as he lay there sobbing in a heap. *I have finally, literally, reached the point of having no possessions, no attachments, no relationships. I have nothing but the clothes on my back. I have hit bottom. It is just me and Nature. This is the point I've been trying to reach all along.* And with that realization, a burst of energy shot through his veins. *I am alive. All those years of wondering whether or not life was worth living, of thinking God had condemned humans to living hell—that was non-sense. I want to live!* The desire was new and exotic, and filled him with power.

Suelo stood. He faced the ice dragon.

"Fuck you, glacier!" he called.

Abandoning his plan of pool-hopping across the ice, Suelo dove headfirst into the river and swam. The current swept him quickly downriver as he kicked his boots and crawled with numb hands. Suddenly, though, his mittened hand scraped rock. Then another rock. He opened his eyes and saw alder brush. He hoisted himself by a branch and wormed onto the shore, panting, weeping, overjoyed.

Ecstatic though he was, Suelo was not yet, as they say, out of the woods. He jogged through the forest to a campground where he found a gathering of gray-haired tourists picnicking beside their motor homes. Breathless and delirious in his soaked woolen rags, Suelo bounded into their site.

"Hello!" he called. "I need help!"

One of the land yachtsmen glanced up from his sandwich, then continued eating.

Wow, thought Suelo, experiencing sudden culture shock. He ran to the next campsite.

"Can you help me?" he cried. No one said a word.

At the third Winnebago, Suelo marched right up beneath the extendable awning, dripping and trembling. "I just came across the glacier, I have hypothermia, my pack is gone, and my friend is across the river and he's going to die. I need help."

With excruciating hesitation, the campers offered him the backseat in their car, fed him a sandwich, delivered him to the lodge, and drove off. Suelo lumbered inside, his toes squishing in his boots. Behind the counter was a hearty sourdough type—mustache, flannel shirt, knife on his belt. He would know what to do. But as Suelo approached, the guy gave him a cold stare.

It was the pilot.

Before Suelo could speak, the man rose in anger.

"You stupid idiot!" cried the man. "That's private property. You have no right being over there."

Suelo slunk back and fell into a chair like a boy in the principal's office.

"All you dipshits from the Lower Forty-eight," lectured the man. "You come up to Alaska for some dickhead adventure and expect us to bail you out when you get in trouble."

Suelo watched the angry lips move but heard nothing. He shriveled. Just minutes before, he'd slain the dragon, swimming that river to save his life, and now he felt like a runt. He recalled his moment of hitting absolute bottom on that hunk of ice. This was worse. In fact, this was worse than death. Would he never put an end to that nagging childhood feeling of being the weakest? Well, if he could stand up to the glacier, he could stand up to this guy.

He lifted his trembling body out of the chair. He walked resolutely toward the man. He inched close enough to smell him, and to drip water onto the wooden counter between them.

"I don't care what you think of me," Suelo said. "I need help. I've got hypothermia and my friend is dying across the river. Whatever you think, put it aside and help me."

Something clicked. The man called his wife to fetch some food and dry clothes. He called a geologist he knew who could operate the cable car. He took Suelo back to the river, and they sent a package of food across the cable, with a note saying to hang tight, that help was on the way. The geologist arrived and brought an elated Ander back in the mining car. He even retrieved Suelo's backpack, which had snagged in a thicket. The lodge owner offered them a place to stay while their stuff dried. The next day the owner went out to the cabin, found Suelo's note of apology, and then apologized himself. He said they'd had trouble with vandals at the cabin, and when he'd seen smoke rising out the chimney from his airplane, he'd assumed Suelo and Ander were the troublemakers.

Safe and warm and dry, Suelo and Ander set out for the Yukon, heading back to the Lower 48. The hero had slain a pair of dragons, another trial on his journey.

"I felt like I was discovering my own manhood," Suelo says a decade later. "First the physical thing with the glacier. Then with the lodge owner. I realized I'm a man and I can talk to a man face-to-face. No man can humiliate me. I felt like it was kind of a late time in life to learn that—but that's when I learned it."

The most important result, however, of Suelo's experiments with nature and chance through 1997 was a deeper analysis of his longtime spiritual hobgoblin: money. "I'm realizing that anything motivated by money is tainted, containing the seeds of destruction," he wrote from Alaska that summer. "That's the struggle—guess that's why Van Gogh couldn't sell his paintings—they had to be pure. There is no honest profession—that's the paradox. The oldest profession [prostitution] is the most honest, for it exposes the bare bones of what civilization is all about. It's the root of all professions."

Part Three

Part Three

11

. . .

Then I saw that all toil and all skill in work came
from a man's envy of his neighbor.
This also is vanity and a striving after wind.

—Ecclesiastes

AT FIRST GLANCE, the late 1990s would seem the oddest of historical moments to become disillusioned with money, for the mere fact that there was so much of it floating around. After the fall of the Soviet Union, capitalism reigned triumphant, and America embraced it more firmly than ever. While the culture wars raged over social issues like homosexuality and abortion, in the realm of economics, there emerged a peculiar consensus. With Bill Clinton as their captain, Democrats rallied to causes that CEOs had championed for decades. Clinton and a Republican Congress united to deregulate industry, reduce the welfare state, and open foreign markets by reducing tariffs. The result of the North American Free Trade Agreement of 1993, the Telecommunications Act of 1996 (to deregulate broadcasting), the Financial Services Modernization Act of 1999 (to deregulate banking)—in concert with the boom in computers and finance—was a historic spike in gross domestic product, stock prices, and corporate profits.

Suelo parted with his final dollars in 2000, the same year that the dot-com bubble peaked, NASDAQ reached its all-time high, and *Forbes* reported, "There's more money at the top than ever before: a combined $1.2 trillion for the 400 richest Americans, up from $1 trillion last year." (If instead of foolishly dropping that thirty dollars in a pay phone, Suelo had bought a plot of dirt—and then cannily sold his nano-acre before the crash—his net worth today might surpass one hundred dollars!) At number one was Bill Gates, whose fortune had topped $101 billion, making him the world's first "centibillionaire." Meanwhile, his business partner, Paul Allen, was about to drop a cool $100 million for a 301-foot, five-story mega-yacht that housed a movie theater and two helicopter pads. Another significant economic event of that year, in addition to the windfall to whoever found Suelo's cash in that phone booth, was the largest corporate merger in history, between Time Warner and America Online, to the tune of $152 billion.

A similar boom had occurred in the Reagan years. But back then, the titans of finance—Ivan Boesky, Michael Milken, Charles Keating, and their ilk—had exuded a whiff of villainy, epitomized by the credo of Hollywood bad guy Gordon Gecko, that greed is good. "In the eighties, maybe, money had been an evil thing," writes the critic Thomas Frank in *One Market Under God*, "a tool of demonic coke-snorting vanity, of hostile takeovers and S&L ripoffs." And throughout that decade, a parade of sourpusses—Jimmy Carter, Walter Mondale, Mike Dukakis, and *their* ilk—had insisted that greed was *not* good, and that the moral thing was to pay higher taxes and wear a sweater indoors when the weather was cold.

Judging by the performance of those candidates at the polls, only a minority of Americans agreed with them. But in the nineties, with the advent of the New Democrats, the opposition to greed seemed to have evaporated altogether. Bill Clinton allowed his party members to straddle a wide chasm—they could still call themselves progressive when it came to fraternizing with gays and listening to Lauryn Hill's latest disc, but also be "fiscally conservative" and support NAFTA, legislation that a decade earlier would have been decried as rank colonialism. Business kings like Gates and Richard Branson and Larry Ellison were lionized. "Our billionaires were no longer slave-driving martinets or pump-and-dump Wall Street manipulators," writes Frank. "They were people's plutocrats, doing without tie and suit, chatting easily with the rank-and-file . . . pushing the stock prices up benevolently this time, making sure we all got to share in the profit-taking."

At the heart of the new consensus was a belief that money itself carried some wisdom. We all want money, went the reasoning, therefore money is good. And if only government with its do-good moralizing would just butt out, we would all prosper. "From Deadheads to Nobel-laureate economists, from paleoconservatives to New Democrats, American leaders in the nineties came to believe that markets were a popular system, a far more democratic form of organization than (democratically elected) governments," concludes Frank.

Any pangs of conscience that liberals might have felt about their unprecedented lucre were allayed by a belief that gracious

America was spreading the wealth far and wide. International agencies like the World Bank and the International Monetary Fund were pumping cash into the Third World to develop agriculture and industry and infrastructure so that all boats might rise with the tide. In 1995, 153 nations formed the World Trade Organization with the goal of greasing the gears of trade, so that even the poorest countries could benefit.

But as the stock market soared and the coffers filled, the consensus began to crack. Critics on both the left and right, from Ralph Nader to Ron Paul, noticed that for all its historic numbers, the bull market wasn't benefiting the average American. Income inequality, which had reached historic lows around 1970, had crept back to levels of the Gilded Age. Eighty percent of the increase in Americans' income between 1980 and 2005 landed in the accounts of the top 1 percent. *BusinessWeek* noted that in 1990, CEOs earned 85 times more than workers; in 1999, they earned 475 times more. Globalization thumped the American farm and factory, wiping out middle-class jobs.

And while it's true that in the 1990s some Americans were taking home more dollars than ever, their raises did not necessarily indicate a larger piece of the pie. Many of the families that maintained the buying power of the previous generation did so not with better jobs, but thanks to the combination of cheap foreign goods and two working parents. The Economic Policy Institute reported that in 1999 Americans worked six weeks more per year than a decade earlier. Full-time jobs with benefits and retirement plans were replaced with temp and part-time that required workers to dig into their paychecks for health insurance and retirement contributions—or forsake them altogether.

As a result, the average personal savings rate slipped into free fall, and in 1999 it dipped into the red; in other words, Americans were now borrowing money to maintain the standard of living that their parents had paid for outright. Those icons of the nineties—shimmering SUVs and sprawling McMansions—were on loan from the bank. Against the tide of historic corporate profits and stock prices, real wages had receded. A majority of people were not lenders but borrowers, whose net worth was zero or negative. The decade's prosperity was a facade.

The first revolt came from the left, in the fall of 1999. A coalition of labor unions, environmentalists, and social-justice advocates took aim at the four-year-old World Trade Organization, which was scheduled to convene in Seattle in November. Deaf to the hoorays about the New Economy spilling from politicians like Clinton and pundits like Tom Friedman, environmentalists mistrusted the WTO. It was, after all, an unelected international body with no legal jurisdiction that had nonetheless succeeded in thwarting laws passed by the elected officials of sovereign nations. For instance, the U.S. Endangered Species Act prohibited American importers from buying shrimp that had been harvested with nets that could accidentally kill sea turtles. Asian nations challenged the law before the WTO, which sided with the shrimpers. America was forced to back down.

Organized labor had its own reason for opposing the meeting. One tenet of the WTO's mission to "liberalize" international trade was to enable corporations to set up shop in other countries. After a century of struggle to establish workplace conditions that we take for granted—a forty-hour workweek, overtime, compensation for job injuries, elimination of child labor—unions saw their jobs vanish as bosses simply shuttered American factories and relocated to Third World countries that had no such laws.

And so it was that on November 30, an odd mix of hard hats and people dressed as sea turtles, with a healthy smattering of jugglers and puppeteers, blocked the streets around the Seattle convention center, not merely protesting the meeting of the WTO ministers, but actually preventing it. It was not only the most powerful blow to date against the globalization free-for-all, but the most successful economics-driven display of civil disobedience in American history.

Surprising as it is that opposition to international monetary policy could bring together longshoremen and tree huggers, what's truly peculiar is that similar antipathies were also aligning those left-leaning groups with the far right. In 1994, a member of the John Birch Society, C. Edward Griffin, self-published *The Creature from Jekyll Island*, a six-hundred-page screed against the Federal Reserve. His thesis is that America's central bank, the Fed, is merely a cartel that with the blessing of Congress has established a legal monopoly that will inevitably bankrupt the United States and all her citizens. Now in its twenty-fifth printing, and translated into Japanese, Vietnamese, and German, the book has become a Magna Carta for gold bugs and Tea Partiers livid about government bailouts and the spiraling national debt. To understand the breadth of the book's appeal, consider that it got blurbs from both Ron Paul and Willie Nelson. When in 2010 I requested a copy from my local public library, I was informed that twenty-five patrons were ahead of me on the waiting list.

Some may cringe at Griffin's discovery of socialist conspiracy in every historical event from the Bull Moose presidential run of Theodore Roosevelt to the sinking of the *Lusitania*, the Crash of

'29, the collapse of the Soviet Union, and the founding of Earth Day. But his plain critique of monetary policy is illuminating and alarming. "The total of this human effort is ultimately for the benefit of those who create fiat money," writes Griffin, with a flourish oddly reminiscent of Karl Marx himself. "It is a form of modern serfdom in which the great mass of society works as indentured servants to a ruling class of financial nobility."

Unlike most modern monetary critics, Griffin begins by addressing the question: what is money? Since its earliest inception, he tells us, money has been a medium of exchange. The barter system, of course, predates money: a poultry farmer might trade a dozen chickens to a grain farmer for a bushel of wheat. As villages became larger and trade more complex, the direct trading of commodities became impractical: try stuffing a dozen chickens in your wallet. So materials such as beads and seashells were used as tokens of barter—money. In the American colonies, tobacco leaves were used as currency: they were durable, lightweight, and easy to transport. Best yet, to avoid losses in an inflationary market, one could merely stop spending and start smoking.

The most permanent of these commodity monies was precious metals. Gold and silver and copper had the advantage of being rare (to ensure the market would not be flooded), nonperishable, and easy to transport, weigh, and divide. The use of metal money lasted for centuries with relative success—and ended only recently. The system's demise, however, began almost at its inception. Once a man amassed more gold than he could safely store at home, he sought a secure vault. For a small fee, he stored his wealth in the warehouse of the goldsmith. When he made his deposit, the proprietor issued a receipt that stated *Pay to the Bearer on Demand.* And thus paper money was born. People soon learned that the paper receipts were equal to their stated worth in gold, and indeed could be redeemed at the vault for gold itself. So it became safe to exchange the currency for goods and services while the gold sat safely in a warehouse.

And here's where the problem started. The goldsmiths realized that they were sitting on a fortune in unused gold. As long as the paper receipts were trusted as money, people rarely redeemed them for gold. By lending out his customers' gold—and charging interest—the clever goldsmith could make additional profit. Hence the ascent of the modern bank. Now let's say the blacksmith deposits one hundred gold dollars, and receives one hundred paper dollars as his receipt. The banker turns around and lends those hundred gold coins to the farmer who, not wanting to lug around a sack of heavy metal, immediately redeposits the coins in exchange for one hundred paper dollars. Suddenly there are twice as many paper dollars as gold coins. If the farmer and the blacksmith arrive at the bank at the same moment demanding coin, they will find only one hundred gold dollars for their two hundred vouchers. By artificially doubling the supply of paper money, the banker has halved its value. The blacksmith and the farmer must now redeem their paper dollars for fifty cents each. Multiply this scenario by a thousand, or a million, and we have a run on the banks. (Also, even though the farmer has lost fifty dollars because of the banker's scheme, he must still pay the banker interest on the full one hundred that he borrowed. The banker tends to win either way.)

This system, in which paper money is worth only a fraction of its stated value in gold or silver, was employed in the United States into the twentieth century. Then Congress created the Federal Reserve, authorized it to print billions of dollars of currency that was not directly bound to gold or silver or any other real commodity. It's a mind-boggling concept, but what it boils down to, says Griffin, is a grand counterfeiting racket. When the economy is stagnant, the Fed simply prints currency and lends it (with interest) to the United States Treasury, which distributes the loot to county and state road departments, to military contractors, and of course, as interest payments to the banks and investors that lent them money the last time around. Hence the national debt. American dollars are not redeemable for actual wealth like, say, the gold bars in the Fort Knox Bullion Depository; they are merely IOUs from the Treasury to the Fed. If Congress needs a trillion dollars, the Fed waves its magic wand and the money appears. There is no need to consult the voters or raise their taxes. Suddenly the money exists, and another trillion dollars is marked in a ledger, added to the national debt.

"What we think is money is but a grand illusion," concludes Griffin. "The reality is debt." In fact, "if everyone paid back all that was borrowed, *there would be no money left in existence.*"

William Greider, political reporter for *The Nation* and *Rolling Stone,* critiques the Fed from the opposite side of the political spectrum in his book *The Secrets of the Temple,* and reaches a similar conclusion: "Above all, money was a function of faith. It required an implicit and universal social consent that was indeed mysterious. To create money and use it, each one must believe and everyone must believe. Only then did worthless pieces of paper take on value."

As our money shifts from metals to currency to credit cards and online transactions, the illusion becomes even more pronounced. "When money is no longer represented even by paper, it becomes a pure abstraction, numbers filed somewhere in the memory of a distant computer," writes Greider. "In the computer it cannot be seen by anyone, neither its owner nor the bank clerk who does the accounting."

Faith notwithstanding, why do we continue to accept these counterfeit dollars, even as their value is decimated by inflation? Because it's the law. The government has mandated that this funny money be legal tender for all debts public and private. It is a *crime* to not accept it. Imagine how you'd be laughed out of the HR office if you demanded your salary not by cash, check, or direct deposit, but in gold bullion. Our type of money, intrinsically valueless but mandated by law as legal tender, is called fiat money, and according to Griffin is the first fissure in the dike of civilization: "The chain of events begins with fiat money created by a central bank, which leads to government debt, which causes inflation, which destroys the economy, which impoverishes the people, which provides an excuse for increasing government power, which is an on-going process culminating in totalitarianism."

Or as Greider puts it: "When a society lost faith in money, it was implicitly losing faith in itself."

. . .

DESPITE HIS LIBERAL politics, Suelo was among those captivated by *The Creature.* "Griffin's book is popular with conservatives, having conservative ideas (that sometimes rub me the wrong way)," Suelo explains. "That's a shame, because it keeps progressives from unearthing its gems. Griffin's book was the final straw that broke the camel's back, convincing me I must go moneyless." His conclusions echo those of the activists blockading the Seattle streets. He agrees that banking is a racket, a criticism that dates to biblical times. The Old Testament condemns usury—the lending of money at interest—and when Jesus discovered moneylenders doing business in the temple, he famously upturned their tables and drove them off, saying, "It is written, My house shall be called a house of prayer: but ye make it a den of robbers." Americans accustomed to paying interest on credit cards and mortgages may be astonished to learn that usury was once considered so pernicious that it was banned by the Catholic Church for more than twelve centuries. William Greider writes that medieval usurers, "though they might be wealthy merchants and prominent in Church affairs, were excommunicated and refused burial in Christian ground, condemned with robbers, prostitutes, and heretics . . . The moral offense was profit without work. The usurer sold time, which belonged only to God." While collecting interest has been accepted in the United States for centuries, the charging of ruinously high rates was prohibited in most states by usury laws that capped them at around 10 percent. Those laws were overturned by the U.S. Congress in 1980—one of the many deregulatory factors that contributed to the top-heavy boom of the following decades.

"If banks went out of business, most world poverty would end," Suelo says. "I really feel that. The way that the system is set up, it causes the goods to flow from the workers to the nonworkers, poor to the rich. That's just the nature of interest banking."

But Suelo's opposition to money goes deeper than believing that usury is a scam. Money, he concludes, agreeing with Griffin and Greider, is but a figment of our imagination—an agreed-upon fairy tale. Which wouldn't be harmful, except that so many people accept it as real. "Money, therefore, contains a continuous illusion of immortal power—the psychic vehicle for defeating time itself by controlling the future," writes Greider.

"No one can be absolutely certain of living beyond the grave, but they know their money will."

This is where Suelo's lifelong debate about the nature of time dovetails with his opposition to money. Just as his fundamentalist parents believed that the tragedy of linear time—our certain deaths—could be thwarted by belief in the Millennium, so do capitalists believe that we can create fortunes that will live forever, through the miracle of compound interest. But because he questions their shared premise, that time travels in a straight line, Suelo rejects both remedies.

"I don't see money as evil or good: how can illusion be evil or good?" he writes. "But I don't see heroin or meth as evil or good, either. Which is more addictive & debilitating, money or meth? Attachment to illusion makes you illusion, makes you not real. Attachment to illusion is called idolatry, called addiction."

Suelo takes his critique a step further. He believes that money is not the disease, just a symptom. Money is merely the most convenient means of keeping track of the much deeper, and timeless, human inclination toward credit and debt.

As Suelo sees it, through his readings of the holy texts as well as the philosophies of Tolstoy, Thoreau, and Gandhi, "All these separate, distant Scriptures and authors agree: the way of truth is the way of nonpossession." Poverty is my pride, says Mohammed. Let us live happily, then, though we call nothing our own, says the Buddha. If you want to be perfect, teaches Jesus, go, sell what you have and give to the poor. As Suelo interprets this: "Basically, the greatest sage is at the very bottom of the social scale—a bum." An enlightened man has freed himself from both debt and credit.

If the prophets agree that truth lies in having nothing, how did a world of professedly religious people stray so far, into a society controlled by banks and interest, credit and debt? "Poverty was once considered a Christian virtue for it was meant to indicate a lack of concern for the values of this world and a concentration on the life to come," writes Vine Deloria in *God Is Red*. "In the centuries after the Protestant Reformation, poverty was considered indicative of sloth and other sins, and it was seen as proof of the individual's degeneracy . . . As the white populace of Christian America has become more affluent, the concept of stewardship has been developed to explain the embarrassingly rapid growth of wealth of a substantial number of peoples. The theory goes that we are not really greedy, God has simply blessed us by giving us wealth over which we are to exercise good stewardship."

In Suelo's mind, the problem is far more ancient than the Fed or the WTO or even the invention of currency. Our reliance on money is akin to Original Sin, or the hubris of Prometheus stealing fire from the gods. "Notice how predators and prey have no sense of vengeance, no pay back. Payment and Debt belong to the Universe, not to individuals. ('Vengeance [Pay-Back] is mine,' says the Lord). Yet we humans have stolen payment and debt from the gods. We cannot freely give or freely receive anything. We live under constant obligation."

It is not this way with any other species. As Suelo learned by living in wilderness, in nature there is no barter. When a grizzly bear gathers raspberries, it doesn't owe anything to the raspberry bush. When a raven picks at the carcass of a deer, it is not indebted to that dead animal, or to its species, or to the predator or automobile that killed the deer in the first place. Similarly, when a bee pollinates a flower, it does not expect payment. In

Suelo's mind, nature operates on a "gift economy": animals freely take what is available and freely give what they have.

This view is problematic to a culture that values work. Humans tend to admire predators like eagles, lions, and bears—we place them as symbols on flags and currency—partly for their power and majesty, but also because they "work" for their meals. We also admire industrious creatures like honeybees and beavers. But you won't see a coyote or vulture or barnacle on a silver dollar. These creatures are scavengers, parasites. They don't give anything back, they don't "work," and therefore by human standards they are lesser beings.

But it gets Suelo to thinking. It's true, the coyote doesn't stockpile carrion for hard times, but neither does he share it with others. He certainly doesn't tithe a portion of his monthly prey to the starving coyotes in Mexico, nor to his famished jackal cousins in Africa. Yet he manages to survive. And he plays as critical a role in nature as the supposedly noble predators. Aren't humans merely projecting their own obsession with work onto the animal kingdom, where, in fact, such a hierarchy of worth doesn't exist?

"All this work, work, work and obligation we think is so righteous is really evil, destructive," Suelo concludes. "The more I read the Sermon on the Mount, the more I see it is instructions for releasing ourselves from the Money System—the System of Debt & Obligation."

. . .

SUELO'S SUMMER LIVING off the land in Alaska in 1997 was his first glimpse that moneylessness was possible. And his trip back to the Lower 48 provided further support. By the time he and

Ander parted ways, Suelo was down to fifty dollars in cash. Attempting as always to test a hypothesis, he set off hitchhiking, wondering if he could make it all the way home on such limited funds. He thumbed his way across the Yukon, through British Columbia, then inland to the Oregon desert to visit Tim Wojtusik. Once again, people amazed him with their generosity: rides, meals, invitations to stay in their homes. And when he finally arrived home in Moab, he counted his cash.

Forty-five dollars.

In two weeks of traveling he'd spent only five bucks. He inventoried what he'd bought. Candy bars. A few cups of coffee. Things that he could have just as easily done without. And suddenly his far-fetched theory seemed an actual possibility.

Yet even as these ideas began to cohere, he was not ready to put them into practice. "I've got to believe this stuff myself," he wrote. "Obviously I don't yet. I still keep losing faith and sliding back into this slavery of obligation." He was not the first idealist to run into this problem. "But even a medicine man like myself has to have some money," writes Lame Deer, "because you force me to live in your make-believe world where I can't get along without it."

Suelo set about wresting himself from money. The first problem was his outstanding student loan. Years before, he had simply stopped making payments. But then a collection agency harassed his parents. They had cosigned for the loan, and if he reneged, his parents, now turning seventy, would be forced to pay. Paying this debt had been one of the first motivations for living without paying rent. This time, upon returning to Moab, he didn't even bother with the ritual of renting a home before chafing and moving out. Instead, he immediately set up camp in the canyon. Rehired at his old job at the shelter, he began chipping away at the principal, often paying double or triple the minimum monthly payment. He also returned to volunteering at Conrad Sorenson's food emporium. "I come down here to the co-op to work for food, not money. It's still reciprocation, but at least it's a step, a weaning of myself from Babylon."

By the following summer, he had paid off his student loan. He reported to Timo, "No bills, no rent, no insurance, no car, no license, no nonsense." He was almost there. Yet something prevented him from taking the final step. He hoped to gain that last bit of resolve by sharing his wisdom with others.

Years earlier, in a letter to his sister, he had declared that writing was his true vocation. Now he finally felt stable enough to tackle it: "I'm still working on my mysteries of the universe treatise or whatever it is." But as clear as the ideas were in his head, it was difficult to get them down on paper. "I want to find this message so clearly that a child can understand it—or a bull-headed adult, yet will at the same time be challenging to the most pragmatic scientist. It's basic Ecology, pure and simple, I'm seeing at the heart of religion."

But try as he might to express his message simply, every attempt came out garbled and confusing. So with the exception of Timo, Suelo didn't tell anyone what he was up to. He recognized that it was extreme, weird, and half-baked. "I keep thinking that I'm going to start sharing these ideas with people, like here in Moab. But I realize how much I'm still a slave to hypocrisy. So I have to go hide in the desert some more, let my backbone develop, strengthen, so I can overcome my spinelessness."

It occurred to him that the problem might be the medium, not the message. "Writing isn't doing it for me," he wrote to Tim

Frederick in 1998. "I need to share with people directly." Suelo decided to present a lecture series at the local recreation center. He rented it for an hour for sixty dollars, and posted flyers all around town. "Common Spiritual Threads in World Religions" was the first installment. Admission cost one dollar.

Even in the run-up to the lecture, he encountered problems. He posted his advertisement on a bulletin board in the post office, but the next day it had been removed. He had pinned it beside a poster for a film festival, and that one was intact. He reposted, and the next day found that it was missing again. Finally he asked the clerk what had happened. She had taken it down because it was a commercial event, she informed him, whereas the film festival was nonprofit.

"But it only costs a dollar," Suelo stammered. "And that won't even cover the cost of the building."

"Rules are rules."

Suelo vowed never to charge money for his ideas again.

The night of the lecture arrived. Suelo arranged the rows of folding chairs. He reread his notes. A few familiar faces trickled in. Still a lot of empty seats. Then: his parents. They'd driven all the way from Fruita. In all, he attracted an audience of five. It was better than nothing. He lectured on Taoism, Buddhism, Hinduism, and Christianity. His parents asked a series of questions—pointed but not argumentative. It went off pretty well. Nonetheless: only five people. He couldn't help but conclude the lecture was a flop. Plus the thing had cost him fifty-five dollars. He never got around to presenting the second lecture.

He grew impatient with ideas in general. "I still get frustrated that much of my philosophies are still just concepts in my head. I need some kind of empowerment, energy. Getting excited about ideas isn't enough. Writing them down isn't enough." Maybe his gift was not to articulate ideas, after all: it was to live them. "The sage makes bum-hood the ultimate art," he wrote. It was clear that his spiritual path would require quitting money. But looking around him, he just didn't see how that could happen. Save for street dregs and wilderness hermits, there was simply no tradition of living without money in the United States.

And so Suelo embarked on the next leg of his journey: he went to the East.

12

. . .

Sacred books only point out the way to God.
Once you have known the way, what is the use of books?

—Sri Ramakrishna

As Suelo was spinning his wheels in Moab in 1998, he came across a book in the co-op library about a nineteenth-century Hindu mystic. Ramakrishna was an uneducated man who fell into semiconscious trances in which he appeared to make contact with God. Many considered him merely insane. Nonetheless, a band of devotees gathered around, convinced that he was an avatar—a divine being in human form. The prophet lived simply, in a temple funded by his followers, the same disciples who would later bring Hinduism to America, establishing the country's first temple in San Francisco in 1906.

Suelo was deeply impressed. One day, according to the biography, a disciple decided to test the master's aversion to money. He hid a rupee under the guru's bed. Presently Ramakrishna returned to his bedroom. "No sooner had he touched the bed than he started back; he had felt the actual physical pain."

Ramakrishna also articulated the futility Suelo suffered

working in charity. "How dare you talk of helping the world?" said Ramakrishna. "God alone can do that. First you must be made free from all sense of self; then the Divine Mother will give you a task to do."

In January of 1999, Suelo left Moab, bound for India. Considering that he would eventually model his life after the Hindu sadhus, it's tempting to assume that, inspired by his readings about Ramakrishna, he set out on an intentional pilgrimage to the master's homeland. In fact, he might never have gone but for an invitation from Michael Friedman, who had spent a semester in India in college and wanted to return for medical research. "Randomness is my guru," Suelo says, and once again he obeyed what it offered, considering the timing of the invitation auspicious. He traveled to Friedman's home in Connecticut. There, the two men bought discounted plane tickets to Thailand, from where they could travel cheaply to India. They planned to spend a couple of months there.

On the eve of their departure, Friedman was delayed by illness. Daniel decided to fly to Bangkok on his own, with Friedman to follow in a month's time. He arrived with a thousand dollars in his pocket, and not knowing a soul or a word of the language. He checked into a rat-infested hostel. "I had a month to kill. I was kind of freaked out."

As with his introduction to Quito a decade earlier, Daniel's first destination was the houses of worship. "The temples are quite beautiful, though I haven't had a chance to see their innards yet," he wrote. This trip marked the end of Daniel's handwritten letters and the beginning of mass emails, which would evolve into the blog. He explained to the recipients, "You are part of an e-list that contains a hodgepodge of friends and family who are pagans, agnostics & atheists, devout Christians, don't-cares, universalists, Buddhists, Quakers, sprinkled with gay, straight, bi, and who knows what else. You each represent a facet of my mind and the contradictions I've sought to resolve within me."

One day he happened upon a popular temple, and quietly sketched a statue of the Buddha in his journal. Although he had studied Eastern religions for years, he had never practiced them. But fresh from his reading of Ramakrishna, he was interested in meditation, and he wondered where a Westerner could learn it. He put the question to an attendant, who directed him to Wat Mahathat, a temple and monastery where practicing Buddhists prayed.

As Suelo plunged into the chaotic streets of Bangkok, he quickly became lost. He raced up and down the streets, no longer looking for the temple, just trying to find his way back to the hostel. As he walked along a tall stone wall, a hidden door swung open, and a monk in orange robes emerged. They almost collided. The monk clutched Suelo by the elbow, steered him through the door, and slammed it. Suelo found himself in a beautiful green garden.

"Where are you going?" said the monk, in good English.

"I'm looking for Wat Mahathat."

"Well," said the monk, smiling and waving his hand across the garden. "You're here."

Suelo was no longer surprised by these sorts of coincidences. Chance had delivered him once again. "My intention, if anything, was to go to India," he says now, "and I wouldn't have thought about that if Michael hadn't asked me. My intention was to observe sadhus, maybe become a sadhu, and delve into Hinduism. But I got swept away by Buddhism."

The monk introduced himself as Adjan Sumeto, and Suelo said he wished to learn to meditate.

"Follow me." Sumeto led him to a bodhi tree—the same kind of tree beneath which the Buddha gained enlightenment—and briefly outlined the religion's Four Noble Truths and Eightfold Path. He said, "Now let's meditate."

The monk sat cross-legged, and Suelo joined him. He didn't know exactly what he was supposed to do, and the monk didn't explain, so Daniel just sat silently for twenty minutes. Then the monk plucked a leaf from the bodhi tree, wrote his name on it, ushered Suelo to the door, and told him to return at five the next morning. Daniel found his way back to the hostel. The next morning the monk led him to a room of Thai people in meditation and said, "There you go." Suelo sat down and imitated the others. He sat through sermons in Thai. "No one seemed too concerned about me," he says.

After a few days of this, another monk asked what he was doing there.

"I'm learning to meditate."

"Who sent you here?"

"Adjan Sumeto."

"Adjan Sumeto? Are you sure?"

"Yes. Adjan Sumeto."

"Is he back in Thailand?"

Suelo related the story of their meeting, producing the signed bodhi leaf as evidence.

"You're very lucky," said the monk. "Many people wait many years to meet Adjan Sumeto. He is the most famous monk in all Thailand."

Suelo never saw the mysterious monk again. However, he

decided to continue his meditation practice. The second monk suggested a monastery more amenable to English speakers, and Suelo took a third-class train to the mountains and enrolled in a monthlong training. He meditated in lotus position ten hours a day. No solid foods were eaten after noon. The teachers forbade extraneous conversation.

Suelo proved a headstrong pupil. Lotus position was so painful, and boring. When after a week he complained to Tanach and Kate, the teachers, Tanach replied, "Ah, you're trying too hard."

"You give me these assignments and instructions and then tell me I try too hard? I'm exhausted and I feel sick."

"That's good," said Tanach. "Mental and physical toxins are coming out."

Suelo was frustrated. One day instead of meditating he lay down and slept. He resented the hierarchy of the place. The monks just stood around smoking and chatting all day while the nuns cooked their meals. During services, the monks sat on the elevated stage, the pupils sat on the floor, and the nuns sat in back. And then the priest talked about how this particular monastery had a direct lineage to the Buddha himself, that it was the only true Buddhism, and the others were frauds. Suelo felt like he was back in the Plymouth Brethren. Three weeks into his training, he packed his bags, stormed into Tanach's office, and announced that he was leaving.

"You forgot to bow to the Buddha."

"I don't want to bow to the Buddha."

"Why?"

"It's just a statue. The only reason I'm doing it is to please you. It's not out of truth, or out of my heart. And besides, bowing to the Buddha is contrary to the teachings of the Buddha."

Tanach considered this for a moment.

"I agree with you," he said. "Maybe you can think that you're bowing to the Buddha within."

Tanach convinced Suelo to stay. The meditation improved. One day he felt bliss, the next day sick and frustrated. "You're learning the impermanence of all things," said Tanach. "Yesterday you were on cruise control, now you're not. That's entering high wisdom."

Then the instructors told Daniel to start reducing his sleep. Stay up later, get up earlier. "That was the hardest part," he says. "I also felt tired, didn't deal well with fatigue. The last thing I wanted to hear was to *sleep less*. But I stuck it out until finally they told me: no sleep at all. Stay awake all night in walking and sitting meditation."

The point of the meditation was to always return to the present moment. That night Tanach gave him a koan—a phrase to meditate upon: "Vow to find what you've never experienced or seen before, or never will again."

As Suelo sat in lotus, thoughts from his long-lost Christianity began to surface. "I started thinking about growing up, my childhood, my feelings, the intense peace I found in my religion: I'd thrown it all out together. But I couldn't deny that intense peace at the core. What touched me at my deepest soul was my own religion." He recalled Jesus's words: "Therefore do not worry about tomorrow, for tomorrow will worry about itself. Each day has enough trouble of its own." Suelo wasn't the first to notice that Christ's teachings about humility, forgiveness, and contemplation were pretty similar to those of the Buddha. And this idea of living in the moment dated back further than either: the word "Yahweh," the Hebrew word for God, translates literally as "the eternal present." Since college, Suelo had known that at their core, all religions tapped the same truths. Now, in deep meditation, he actually *felt* it. But his training was not finished.

"After the first night, I said I'm glad that's over," Suelo says. "The next night they told me to stay awake again. They told me to tabulate every time I nodded off. They call it rising and falling. They wanted me to focus on that, to make little marks every time I did that. All these assignments. Another phrase. I was getting so tired, and sick of it. This is so much effort. It's just not natural. I was trying to tabulate in the lotus position, half the night or more. Finally I just took the scrap of paper and slid it aside. I couldn't sit in lotus anymore. The hell with it all. I got out of lotus and slumped, head on my knee.

"And suddenly everything went silent. Complete bliss. Everything turned blank and blue. Except I saw a person with his head on his knee. Who is that? Is it me, or the Buddha? I didn't know who it was. Complete silence. Blue light. No feeling, no thought, no anything. And I thought: 'I have to go back.' I wasn't sure why. I lifted my head up and I was back in the room. I could hear every chirp outside. I got up and felt I'd had the best sleep of my life, so energized and awake.

"I started laughing. I almost felt like someone was watching me. It was a trick, all these hoops and games, to make me quit. Because that's what it's about—that moment of giving up. Wow. It was so funny. I laughed out loud. I started walking around the monastery, pitch-black, quiet as ever, and I was laughing. I thought, 'Well that's it. This is what I came here to learn.' The whole idea of going through all these nonsense things made sense. They were supposed to be nonsense. If you don't go through the nonsense, you won't realize it's nonsense, therefore it's not nonsense.

"Anyway, I went back to my cubicle. That whole month we weren't supposed to take showers. There was a little shower. I jumped in and cleaned up. There were a couple hours before five. I slept. I awoke and felt great. Jumping and skipping. I went to my instructors. Kate was there. How did your night go? I had a big smile. I told her. I thought she would be happy for me. She had this grave look on her face. Tanach came out and sat down. They whispered to each other.

"Then Tanach said, 'Well, this wasn't supposed to happen this early. You're very lucky. But this might be very hard. Not very many people get to experience this. You might try to regain this, and that will make your road difficult. This is about the present moment. If you keep thinking back and trying to regain this, it will be hard. Now it's dangerous. We actually wanted you to stay awake one more night. You weren't supposed to shower and go to bed. But that's fine, you can leave now, or stay another night. It's up to you. It doesn't matter.' He seemed kind of happy for me.

"I stayed another night. Stayed awake. I felt really good. In the middle of the night I was doing walking meditation when Tanach showed up. That was the first time anyone ever came to the cubicle. He came in. As I was walking and meditating, he said, 'It's like time doesn't matter anymore. When you're walking you can't tell if it's been an hour or five minutes.'"

Were Joseph Campbell narrating Suelo's story, he might say that the hero had reconciled with God. He had found the eternal present—and unlike the hell of his poison-berry vision a decade before, this time it was heaven. "The hero has died as a modern man," writes Campbell, "but as eternal man—perfected, unspecific, universal man—he has been reborn."

Suelo knew that he had been through a life-changing experience, but wasn't sure what to call it. "I never had any intention of becoming part of any religion, or calling myself anything," he says. "I just wanted to explore the depths of Buddhism. To take the truth out of every religion. Run with it."

Paradoxically, what he found at its depths was Christianity. "So I thought: 'I have to embrace what in it is true, and throw out what is not, instead of throwing it all out.' The only reason I wouldn't is because I'm worried about what people think, and part of that is I don't want to be associated with the hypocrites. It's that way for a lot of people. Is it possible to embrace the truths we've been given, accept what's good in our roots, and not become hypocritical, like this fear that I would become a crazy fundamentalist?"

Suelo's first inclination after leaving the monastery was to go to India and become a sadhu. After Michael Friedman arrived in April, the two men flew to Calcutta and crossed the nation by third-class train, visiting the temples of the Buddha, Ramakrishna, and Mother Teresa. Daniel met some sadhus, who live today much as they have for centuries. They own nothing, dwell in caves or forests or temples, and survive on the alms of others. These men are naked or wrapped in just a loincloth, with long beards and dreadlocks. They often cover their bodies with ash and paint their faces brightly. To demonstrate their lack of attachment to their physical bodies, they might perform acts of physical suffering like lying on a bed of spikes or holding their hands overhead for days at a time.

Suelo quickly learned that not even holy men were free of the tentacles of money. Many of those calling themselves sadhus were frauds, bilking visitors for cash to show them fake relics or perform bogus ceremonies. Suelo's reaction was like that of Gandhi, who reported after a visit to the shrines: "I came to observe more of the pilgrims' absentmindedness, hypocrisy, and slovenliness, than of their piety. The swarm of sadhus, who had descended there, seemed to have been born but to enjoy the good things of life." Suelo even met a European sadhu, and spent a few days with him. But upon discovering that the man kept a Swiss bank account, into which he'd occasionally dip when he wanted a respite from poverty, Suelo was disillusioned. The Indian temples seemed not so much like sacred spaces as a racket overrun with charlatans. Suelo scolded guides and cabdrivers as they delivered him to a cousin's teahouse to spend money. When an innkeeper promised not to sell Suelo anything and then took him to a silk shop, Suelo exploded.

"I don't want to buy anything," he sputtered, sweating from a fever and the summer heat. "I have very little money, and I'm tired of getting scammed. Everywhere I go in India someone is trying to scam me. And this is Varanasi, supposed to be the holy city of God, and all I've seen is corruption and greed, and children working in sweatshops, and I don't want to support that."

Suelo demanded the man take him back to the hotel, and started packing up his stuff, while the innkeeper begged him to stay. Suelo flayed the man with lines from the Bhagavad Gita: "The Scriptures say to renounce the fruits of your actions, to not expect things in return, to give freely!"

Remorse clouded the innkeeper's face. He wept. "Please stay," he cried. "I'm sorry. I won't do it again."

But Suelo was delirious and stubborn. "I have to keep my word.

I told you that if you tried to sell me something I was leaving the hotel, and I'm keeping my word. Keep your word to people from now on if you want to make amends." And with that, the hero stomped off on shaky legs into the squalor, looking for a new hotel.

Fleeing the June heat and the scams, he parted ways with Friedman and rode a bus to the Himalayas, to an outpost of Tibetan Buddhists. He rented a room from a Hindu family in "a slate-shingled mud house with no running water on a slope of a mountain, in a group of houses called Dharamkot, above a town called Bagsu, above the larger town of McLeod Ganj, way above the even larger town of Dharamsala." He loved the cool rainy mountains. "All around my place are terraced, cultivated fields stepping down the steep slopes," he wrote. "And there are monkeys everywhere! (You've probably figured out by now that I love monkeys.)"

He continued studying Buddhism for a month while volunteering to tutor a monk in English. "Tibetans are incredibly peaceful, happy, down-to-earth people—more so than any other people I've encountered," he wrote. "You go to the temples and monasteries and find so much joviality, but not to the exclusion of intense sincerity. There's so little or no self-righteousness & pretension & pompousness that is so common in every other religion I've witnessed."

The monk gave him a book about Milarepa, the twelfth-century Tibetan saint. It was heady stuff, not for the novice: "First, concerning the conquest of non-human beings: the Master gave the Demon King Binayaka at the Red Rock of Chonglung the teaching on the Six Ways of Being Aware of One's Lama." Yet Suelo was captivated. When Milarepa took to the caves, he made this vow:

So long as I have not attained the state of spiritual illumination,

I will not descend to enjoy alms, or offerings dedicated to the dead, even if I die of hunger in this mountain solitude.

I will not descend for clothing even if I die of cold.

I will not indulge in worldly pleasures and distractions, even if I die of sadness.

I will not descend to seek medicine, even if I die of sickness.

Without allowing myself to be distracted in body, speech, and mind, I will work to become Buddha.

What's more, here was a holy man who dwelled in not one cave but twenty! Suelo hiked into the mountains to camp in these legendary alcoves, each with its own name: Horse Tooth White Rock and Shadow of the Pleiades, Ragma Cave of Enlightenment and Banner of the Sky, Sensory Pleasure of Betse and Lonely Cuckoo. Such mystery and poetic power—a cave was not just some dank hole in the rock, it was the Lotus of the Grotto!

Although disappointed by the sadhus, Suelo was still wondering if he should remain in the East. Upon returning to Dharamsala, he learned that the Dalai Lama was in town, and went to hear him.

"All you Westerners," said the Dalai Lama. "It's admirable that you come all this way to learn Tibetan Buddhism. But the grass is always greener on the other side of the fence. Every culture and every religion teaches truth. And we always think the other culture's is better than our own. It's good for some of you to learn Tibetan Buddhism and become monks, but it's not for everyone. Most of you are looking for something other than where you're at. I'd recommend that most of you go back to your own cultures, learn your own wisdom, your own traditions."

Suelo knew this was right. He'd come all this way, crossed oceans and deserts and climbed mountains to sit at the feet of the Lama himself, only to learn that what he needed was to go home. That was the purpose of his time in the monastery—to rediscover the faith of his youth. He had been cut off from his roots, and now he needed to return. "The irony is that my aim in exploring other faiths has been to learn more about Christianity," he wrote at the time, "not to become a Buddhist or Hindu or whatever." There was a pressing emotional need to return, too: if he quit money in India, he would never see his family again. That was too sorrowful a prospect to bear. Finally, Suelo just wasn't interested in leading the cloistered life of a monk. As much as he admired the Tibetans, he quibbled with their theology, complaining about "the common tendency of Buddhists and Christians to see the world as an evil to escape from."

Suelo wanted to engage the physical world, even with all its trials and corruption. "I wanted to be a sadhu," Suelo says. "But what good would it do for me to be a sadhu in India? A real test of faith would be to go back to one of the most materialistic, money-worshipping countries on earth and be a sadhu there."

· · ·

AND SO BEGAN the final phase of our hero's journey: Return. "His second solemn task and deed therefore is to return then to us, transfigured, and teach the lesson he has learned of life renewed," writes Campbell. "The first problem of the returning hero is to accept as real, after an experience of the soul-satisfying vision of fulfillment, the passing joys and sorrows, banalities and noisy obscenities of life. Why re-enter such a world? Why attempt to make plausible, or even interesting, to men and women consumed with passion, the experience of transcendental bliss? As dreams that were momentous by night may seem simply silly in the light of day, so the poet and the prophet can discover themselves playing the idiot before a jury of sober eyes. The easy thing is to commit the whole community to the devil and retire again into the heavenly rock-dwelling, close the door, and make it fast."

Indeed, having decided against the heavenly rock dwelling in the Himalaya, Suelo would find his faith tested by his return to the world's banality. At the time, he didn't see himself as heroic anyway, nor did his life resemble a meaningful journey. He was just confused. He spent another entire year mired in indecision. Once again broke, he camped on Damian Nash's couch for the winter and resumed working part-time at his same old job. He helped his Alaska friend Leslie Howes move to Seattle, and heard her reports of being teargassed at the WTO demonstration. He applied for a permanent full-time job at the women's shelter but didn't get it.

And then Suelo suffered what would be the final indignity of his life with money. He still owned a car, a dented Honda hatchback on whose white flanks he'd painted a flock of black ravens. On a trip to Boulder to visit Tim Frederick, the old car gave up the ghost. Suelo nursed it into a Honda dealership for a diagnosis. The mechanic reported that it needed a new timing belt, a repair that at six hundred dollars cost more than the car was worth. Suelo declined, sure he could find a cheaper mechanic. Maybe his brother could do it for free. Whatever, said the mechanic. But Suelo still owed seventy-five dollars for the diagnosis.

"That's unethical," Suelo argued. "You didn't tell me you were going to charge me just to look at it."

"That's our policy," said the mechanic.

Tim Frederick offered his credit card, happy to help his friend out of this dilemma.

"Put your wallet away," Suelo said. He was fighting this one on principle, the same reason he checked out of that Varanasi hotel. The stalemate continued, with Suelo getting more agitated. Another mechanic stepped forward with a solution. He would take the wreck off Suelo's hands for a hundred dollars. But accepting money seemed like prostitution, an act complicit in the dealership's unethical behavior. Daniel didn't want their money. He wanted them to be honest.

"You can just have the car," he said finally, storming out of the office. It would be the last time he owned a motor vehicle.

Two weeks later, he was back on the road, hitchhiking across the country, visiting friends, living on the cheap. The only way for him to live ethically in this corrupt world, he felt—the only way to access that eternal present that he'd found in the monastery—was to abandon money. Suelo wanted neither to owe nor to be owed. In the words of Christianity, he wanted the Lord to forgive him his debts, and he forgave his debtors. In the words of the Bhagavad Gita, he wanted to release himself from the fruits of his labor. To give freely without expectation of receiving. Only then could he break free of the Western concept of linear time. Credit and debt kept us fixated on the past and the future. In the words of the Buddha, Suelo wanted to cut the tangle of attachments, to break the circle of reincarnation and dwell in the eternal present.

But to just stop using money was not easy. He would have to give up not only most material comforts, but also the freedoms he was accustomed to: driving a car required a license that cost money; traveling abroad required a passport that cost money.

But that was the point. We'd become so entangled that there appeared to be no way out but total refusal. Giving up money might even turn out to be illegal: what if, for instance, he owed back taxes? What he was proposing was a prolonged act of civil disobedience. Suelo was afraid to go it alone.

He learned about a communal farm in Oregon. Members grew crops and shared meals, no money required. Maybe such a place would be right for him. Suelo fired off a couple of emails inquiring if he could come, but received no reply. So he shouldered his pack and thumbed to Eugene, arriving at a ramshackle old house on a sprawling farm.

"I sent an email," he said. "I'm here."

Nobody remembered any email. If he wanted to stick around, they said, sure, go ahead, get to work. They required forty hours per week. That seemed fair. But the work wasn't all digging potatoes and sharing the abundance. A lot of it was busywork—pulling dandelions or sweeping the drive or raking leaves. And the residents weren't actually growing enough food to subsist on—the daily crop could hardly produce a salad. The farm survived from business ventures—they ran a café in the nearest town, and they contracted with the post office to deliver mail. The commune was beholden to credit and debt.

Worse yet, it just wasn't fun. The people were dour and gloomy. Everyone worked their forty hours, and if you were caught idling, you were guilted into working more. It seemed the point of all the work wasn't to produce more crops, but just to keep busy, to avoid being pegged as lazy, a subproductive member. These utopians seemed to have chucked the Protestantism but kept the work ethic.

Suelo thought about the Kung bushmen. They lived in one of

the harshest places on earth, yet they only had to work two hours a day. The rest of the time they spent in leisure. Yet here he was, slaving away on this farm, which was situated in one of the most fertile areas of the planet. What was wrong with this picture?

After a few weeks, Suelo packed his bag and left. The tangle of attachments remained tangled. He hitched up to his sister's house north of Seattle. Now back with her husband, and as firm a fundamentalist as ever, Pennie did not approve of Daniel's drift from Christianity, but she was willing to engage him in conversation about faith and the search for meaning. He took stock of his life. Suelo was thirty-nine years old, six years older than Christ upon crucifixion, six years older than Martin Luther was when he posted the 95 Theses, the same age as Martin Luther King Jr., at the time of his assassination. And what did he have to show for himself? A few adventures abroad. A few years in a cave. Do-gooder jobs.

He had to make a decision. Down one path was gainful employment, a regular life with a roof overhead, bills, debts, and all the moral compromises that came with it. Down the other path lay the romantic quest that beckoned, hatched in deep wilderness, in deep prayer, at the feet of the Lama. This was the path of the heroes and the prophets. But wasn't it just a fantasy? Who was he, Daniel Shellabarger, of Grand Junction, Colorado, to single-handedly reject the modern era? It was a path filled with alienation, hardship, ridicule. Maybe he should give up this fandango. Maybe he should just bear down and get a job. The year was 2000, and the economy was booming. The temptation was great. At the moment it was irresistible.

With his fluent Spanish and Peace Corps résumé, he found a job in Seattle as an advocate for Spanish speakers navigating government bureaucracies. On the first morning, commuting in his sister's car, he sat in traffic for two hours. And then he stepped into chaos. The phone wouldn't stop ringing. Strangers jabbered Spanish in his ear. He had to ask them to repeat themselves—his Spanish was a bit rusty. Stacks of paper spread across the desk in his cramped cubicle. Sweat soaked his shirt. His boss took a look at him and asked if he was sure that this job was what he wanted. He stared back, unable to answer. When six o'clock mercifully arrived, Suelo stumbled out to the street and found a parking ticket slapped on the windshield of his sister's car. He inched up the freeway, another two hours in gridlock. He looked around at his fellow commuters. Not a single one was smiling. Not a single one looked content.

When he finally walked through the door, his sister asked how the day had gone. Daniel erupted: "This is insanity. I don't see how people live like this." He called his new boss, got voice mail, left an apology for wasting her time, regretted that he wouldn't be back.

Now he was sure that he had to complete his journey. He pored over a directory of intentional communities, hundreds of them the world over. But most compromised, took part, through commerce or barter or membership investment, in this insane system he was determined to escape. That wouldn't do. He had to go all the way.

He found a place: the Gandhi Farm, a radical vegan organic cashless off-the-grid commune far in the backwoods of Nova Scotia. Its twenty acres nourished a forest of sugar maple and white birch and quaking aspen, an orchard of walnut and cherry and apple. Plots of wild native strawberries and blackberries and Juneberries ripened in summer. Clear water sprang from a well.

An eighty-year-old farmhouse could sleep eighteen. Eden. The place was so off the grid, in fact, that it didn't have a telephone number or email address.

Daniel looked at a map. Nova Scotia was a long way from Seattle. He had a few hundred dollars left. In September 2000, he bought a bus ticket to Bar Harbor, Maine. The ride lasted five days, the Greyhound cramped and stuffy and stinking of sweat and tobacco and vomit. When he arrived, he hitched to Canada and bought passage on a ferry across the Bay of Fundy. He had fifty dollars left. He folded it in half, then in quarters, and slipped it into his back pocket: his emergency insurance against the occurrence of some Bad Thing, whatever it might be.

Nobody on the ferry would even look at him, much less smile or say hello. He wondered if he smelled bad from the bus trip. He had never felt so unwelcome. Disembarking in Nova Scotia, he started to hitchhike. No one picked him up. He stood there all day. Did he look strange, or dangerous? Finally an old Christian couple stopped for him. He told them about his quest, and they seemed to understand. They took him all the way to the final spur road, wishing him the best.

Only ten more miles. Daniel began walking on the dirt road and put out his thumb. An occasional car passed him but none even slowed down. The woods became deeper and darker. Children playing in the yards of farmhouses scurried behind trees when they saw him. He walked and walked and walked, pack straps digging into his shoulders and his heels rubbing to blisters.

It was dusk when he reached the private road to Gandhi Farm. Naked maple branches hung low over a carpet of brown leaves. Despite the bad vibe he'd gotten all day, he was still thrilled. But when he rounded the final bend and the farmhouse came into view, a shudder raced down his spine. The hulking Victorian farmhouse was a black silhouette against the twilight, windows smashed and curtains shredded to ribbons whipping in the wind. It looked like something out of a Stephen King movie. He took a few steps backward, reassured himself. Finally he climbed the steps to the porch. Shards of glass crunched beneath his boots. The planks creaked. The door hung open on battered old hinges, groaning in the wind.

"Hello?" he called. "Anybody home?"

Just the groan of the hinges and the whistle of the wind and the flutter of the curtains.

"Is anyone here?" he called out. The hair on his neck stood up.

He pushed through the door. He flipped a light switch but it was dead. He tore through his backpack for a flashlight, panting for breath. He swept the beam across the room. Not much to see. He found the remains of an old ledger. He recognized the name of the farm's founder in the scrawl. *October 21, Philip's parents came by to pick up his belongings.* No more entries. More than a month of empty lines on the page. Upstairs he found a wall calendar inscribed with someone's scribbling. *August 21. Dug for water but well is dry. August 22. Dug for water but well is dry. August 23. Dug for water but well is dry.* This went on for weeks.

Suelo wanted to flee, but it was cold and dark and he had nowhere else to go, so he spread his sleeping bag on a cot and lay down. He didn't sleep much. At first light he packed his bag. He lifted his boot and took a step down the road. Then another. Again he walked all day with no rides.

At dusk someone stopped. "I saw you on my way to work," said the driver. "Now I'm on my way home, and you haven't gotten very far. No one's going to pick you up out here." The man went out of his way to drive him to the nearest town.

Daniel considered the fifty dollars in his pocket. If this wasn't the Bad Thing, it would do until one came along. Now what the hell was he going to do? With a glimmer of hope, he fired off an email at the public library to a guy he knew in Halifax. Within a few days they had met up, and his friend said there was this girl, Lorelei, he wanted Daniel to meet. A kindred spirit.

And sure enough, it was like he and Lorelei had known each other forever. She was a fiery redheaded sprite who had been living on the road for years. She talked about past lives and energy and harmony with plants and animals. Turned out she had spent some time at Gandhi Farm the previous year. So Daniel didn't feel self-conscious about telling her his quest.

"I want to live without money," he said.

"Me, too!" she said.

Off they went. With enough faith, the universe would provide. It was dangerous—an urban and industrial landscape, with "No Trespassing" signs everywhere you looked, far from his wide-open canyons and mountains. But the rides came easy. People were much more likely to pick you up when you were traveling with a girl. Maine, New Hampshire, Massachusetts, Connecticut, New York. Oh, it was glorious, tumbling southward with the falling leaves. "Life has been magical for us," he wrote. "Fantastic things happen when you're at the mercy of chance! One couple who picked us up told us all they asked is that we do something for somebody else. They said this is a concept few understand, but that it is most important."

And then at a truck stop on some Pennsylvania highway, he

crossed the final threshold. He and Lorelei had been waiting for two hours with no luck. Flurries of snow swirled in the gloom. His coat was thin. Rows of big rigs rumbled in the parking lot, rainbow splotches of diesel seeped across the asphalt, paper soda cups lay flattened beneath tire tracks in the slush. Once again, anxiety threatened, this worry about some imminent Bad Thing. The Bad Thing that only money could remedy.

Suelo removed the fifty dollars from his pocket. He went into the truck stop, spent a dollar on a stamp and envelope, and mailed twenty dollars to his sister—he still owed her for that parking ticket. His final debt was paid.

He returned to the parking lot. Motorists came and went, pumping gasoline into their vehicles and pouring coffee into themselves. Suelo regarded this scene of mundane commerce with agitation. As he sank deeper into concentration, he felt a growing thrill, as if some revelation were near.

And it hit him: the fifty dollars was not the *cure* for his anxiety, the fifty dollars was the *cause* of it. The Bad Thing would happen, sure. No amount of money, not fifty dollars, or a million, could keep it at bay. Because after all, what was the worst Bad Thing? Death. Mortality. The End of Time. That was the thing he was afraid of. But the Bad Thing came to everyone eventually, and when it arrived, not even money could buy it off.

Money perpetuated the fantasy of immortal earthly life, the illusion that we could determine the future. Suelo was ready to reject this illusion once and for all. The fifty dollars was merely keeping him from what he needed most: faith. If he wanted to know true faith, he had to accept that there was nothing in the material world to fall back upon. Faith was the only salvation from the Bad Thing. So let it happen. "If we embrace holy poverty very closely," said Saint Francis, "the world will come to us and will feed us abundantly." If Suelo believed that Providence would carry him safely, then it didn't matter what came next. He would be fine, with or without a bit of cash in his pocket.

He took his last thirty dollars into a phone booth and left it there, folded it on top of the telephone.

"Somebody has to take the first step to escape from servitude of money," he would later write. "Digging a tunnel out of the prison, and then showing fellow prisoners that life outside the prison is abundant, without judging the fellow prisoners—that is the challenge."

Suelo turned and walked across the parking lot, leaving the money behind.

The heavens broke open. It was mere rain, but to Suelo it felt like something warmer than honey pouring over his head and coursing down his shoulders. He stood paralyzed in ecstasy, embraced by grace, by the love that flows freely across the cosmos. Forgive our Debts, Cut the Tangle, Break the Circle. And when the baptism was over, when the tingling subsided in his trembling limbs, he knew he had arrived in the right place.

It doesn't matter where I am, he now knew. *Wherever I am, I'm at home.*

13

. . .

another year is gone
a traveler's shade on my head,
straw sandals at my feet

—Basho

IN 1953 A woman set off on foot from Los Angeles with nothing but a toothbrush and a sheaf of leaflets calling for an end to all war. Dressed in a plain blue tunic with PEACE PILGRIM printed on the front, the woman, who would not give her birth name, crisscrossed the country for three decades, walking more than twenty-five thousand miles before she stopped counting. Peace Pilgrim never earned or spent money, relying on people she met for food and shelter. Sometimes she went days without food, and slept by the side of the road.

Those like Suelo who imitate Peace Pilgrim's most radical version of the simple life generally do so alone or in very small numbers. A German woman named Heidemarie Schwermer has lived without money for fourteen years, and an Irish man named Mark Boyle has been moneyless for two. Suelo traveled for a few months with a band of Jesus Christians who call themselves a "live-by-faith, work-for-God-not-money Christian community." Despite the similarities, one would be hard-pressed to argue that a handful of moneyless individuals constitutes a movement.

That said, the spectrum of those who practice voluntary simplicity is wide, and not all do it alone. In 2000—the same year Suelo quit money—a punkrocker calling himself "koala" outlined an emerging anticonsumerist philosophy in a pamphlet titled "Why Freegan?" "If you are an anti-capitalist," he wrote, "what better way to protest the economy than withdrawing from it and never using money?" The pamphlet offered tips on dumpster diving, shoplifting, squatting, and foraging, and concluded, "There are two options for existence: 1) waste your life working to get money to buy things that you don't need and help destroy the environment or 2) live a full satisfying life, occasionally scavenging or working your self-sufficiency skills to get the food and stuff you need to be content, while treading lightly on the earth, eliminating waste, and boycotting everything."

Freegans, like the WTO protesters of 1999, were reacting to boundless consumption and ecological waste. The website freegan .info defines the goal as "a total boycott of an economic system where the profit motive has eclipsed ethical considerations and where massively complex systems of productions ensure that all the products we buy will have detrimental impacts most of which we may never even consider. Thus, instead of avoiding the purchase of products from one bad company only to support another, we avoid buying anything to the greatest degree we are able."

By decade's end, the ethos had gained enough adherents to be identified as a movement, particularly in coastal cities like San Francisco, Portland, and New York. Freegans are the latest in a tradition of radical simplicity dating back to the Shaker colonies of the eighteenth century and to Thoreau and the Transcendentalists in the nineteenth century. Its modern practitioners vary widely. In the 1940s, a band of nude long-haired young men known as Nature Boys roamed the canyons of Southern California, sunbathing, sitting in lotus, and browsing raw fruits and vegetables. In the 1960s, a San Francisco anarchist group called the Diggers—they took their name from the seventeenth-century radical communitarians—opened free stores and gave away food and medicine. Each year since 1972, busloads of hippies have congregated on public lands for Rainbow Gatherings, weeklong spiritual and artistic celebrations in which the exchange of money is forbidden. Abbie Hoffman's 1970 manifesto, *Steal This Book,* preached revolution through free food, housing, and transportation: "In a country such as Amerika, there is bound to be a hell-of-a-lot of food lying around just waiting to be ripped off." In 1981, a band of antinuclear protesters collected and served vegetarian food at a protest in Harvard Square beneath a banner demanding FOOD NOT BOMBS. The loosely affiliated group has since disseminated the message—and the meals—worldwide.

In 2007, a young man named Brer Erschadi hitched into Moab. A native of Oklahoma, he had cooked and served at Houston's Food Not Bombs, and thought Moab was ripe for something similar. By then Conrad Sorenson's freewheeling food co-op had folded, replaced by a retail food store, and the town lacked an off-market food source. Working with his new girlfriend, Heila Habibi, Erschadi rode his bike around to restaurants, asking for leftover food.

"What group are you with?" they asked, raising an eyebrow at this lanky bearded fellow with size-fourteen shoes towing a wooden cart behind his junker. When he replied that he was working on his own, he got mostly slammed doors. "We asked for donations from churches but no church would help us," he says today. "Didn't want us in their kitchen."

Brer and Heila were not easily discouraged. "Our first free meal was straight out of the dumpster," he says. On a spring day in 2008, he and Heila hauled their grub back to the shack they shared with five other people and began cooking. There was a sense of urgency—the place didn't even have a fridge, and the food was already ripe. They cooked up a pot of soup and tossed a salad. Then they loaded up the bike carts and rode to the corner of Main and Center and commandeered the sidewalk.

"We didn't have tables or chairs or cars," he remembers. "We set the pots on concrete. Twelve people came. It was really fun and inspired."

Tourists and passersby looked on with curiosity at the ragged band of bean-eaters. Those in attendance were rock climbers and transient kids. Erschadi is as handsome as a movie star, and with his flecks of gray hair and the gangly body of a teenager, it's hard to determine his age. Heila is also a stunning beauty, and has the same black hair and olive skin as Brer—both of their fathers were born in Tehran. Parked on a sidewalk in rural Utah, they were downright exotic. A cop asked some questions, but as soon as he found they weren't charging money, he backed off. "He had a bowl of potatoes with us and went on his way," says Erschadi, who had been hassled by plenty of Houston cops at Food Not Bombs.

"I was actually aching for a confrontation," he admits now. "I was pretty angry at the time. I wanted to unload on someone."

He would get his chance. The first meal was a success, and they made it a regular gig, collecting more cooks and dumpster divers and regular diners. Then one day the health inspector asked to see their permit. Erschadi announced that he didn't need a permit because he was merely having a potluck. The inspector insisted.

"If I have two peanut-butter-and-jelly sandwiches in my backpack," said Erschadi, "and go on a hike and want to give one to my girlfriend, do I need to get your fucking permission?"

The health inspector decided not to push his case with a crew of irate anarchists. "He told me I had to call some number and apply for such and such permit," says Erschadi. "But I never did."

When Brer and Heila had a baby, a firefighter named August Brooks took over Free Meal. His connections to civic leadership brought new legitimacy. Restaurants and even the school cafeterias donated food. Throughout 2009 and 2010, volunteers collected and served a meal every single day, rain or shine or snow.

Free Meal was revolutionary in its simplicity. All the food that would otherwise crowd the landfill instead ended up in people's bellies. No one was turned away. No money changed hands. The food varied day to day from marginal (elementary school cafeteria pork and beans) to passable (day-old pizza) to inspired (prime rib and potatoes.) Unlike Food Not Bombs, Free Meal was not vegetarian. They would eat anything, as long as it had been discarded and was headed for the landfill. The program accepted no cash donations and no purchased food.

"People think this is a soup kitchen, but it's not," August Brooks says. "This is about getting people from all walks of life together."

Indeed, what sounds radical on paper felt more like a picnic: a friendly gathering of all sorts of people, from homeless drifters to nine-to-fivers on their lunch breaks. The unintended consequence of choosing not to eat one's *own* food, in home or office or restaurant, was the fellowship of sharing a meal with strangers, of making new friends.

"People get a meal out of it, but that's not why they come," says Suelo. "They're craving a social interaction that's just gone from most of our society. It feels like real community."

I agree. I had found that as I gained some semblance of financial independence, I'd begun to miss the community I'd created when I had less. Throughout my twenties, my goals were minimal consumption and maximum freedom. I worked part-time seasonal jobs and spent the rest of the year traveling and writing. I earned so little money that I hardly paid taxes. All of my possessions fit inside a truck. I lived communally, not exactly by choice, but because I couldn't afford my own place. During guiding season, I camped out for weeks at a time with teenagers, only to return for days off at a crusty staff house where, if I wasn't lucky enough to score a bunk, I unrolled my sleeping bag on the floor.

I loved this life. But as the years rolled on, I found myself yearning for my own space. When I was thirty-five I finally got it: I bought a small house on a tree-lined street where, for the first time, the room where I wrote was not the same as the one in which I slept. Although I lacked collateral and income, I qualified for a loan at low interest. I worked from home, no longer forced to leave my castle to earn money.

The costs of living the dream, however, were great, and I don't just mean the mortgage, property tax, home insurance, utility bills, health insurance, and retirement savings. I lost the freedom I'd had to stop paying rent and spend a few months in the truck. But the most surprising by-product of my economic independence was this: I was lonely. I became restless and anxious. I yearned for the inconveniences of having to put up with other people.

Study after study shows that the accumulation of wealth and goods is accompanied by a decrease in happiness. And so it's no surprise that in the boom decades, the spectrum of those drawn, like me, toward a simpler life has widened. The ideas put into radical practice by Suelo have also seeped into the mainstream. Amid the decade's economic convulsions, you didn't have to be an anticapitalist to surmise that the system wasn't working. In 2001, the dot-com bubble segued into the real-estate bubble, and easy credit enabled more buying while masking the financial risk. Between 2005 and 2009, publishers brought out no fewer than four books with the title *Affluenza*—defined in a PBS documentary as the "epidemic of overconsumption." Other alarming titles included *The Overspent American: Why We Want What We Don't Need* (1999), *The High Price of Materialism* (2002), and *Born to Buy: The Commercialized Child and the New Consumer Culture* (2005).

At the same time Americans began to think more critically about the things they were buying. Bin Laden's attacks made it harder to ignore how America's dependence on oil financed the very regimes and ideologies that sought to destroy us. Decades of human-caused ecological catastrophes—the Exxon *Valdez* oil spill, the Chernobyl nuclear meltdown, depletion of the ocean fisheries, deforestation of the Amazon—had revealed that the ultimate costs of food and energy were much higher than their bargain price at the register. The devastating effects of our fossil-fuel binge leaped to the international forefront in 2006 when Al Gore's *An Inconvenient Truth* became a box-office smash and won him a Nobel Peace Prize. Even those disinclined toward guilt over getting ten miles to the gallon, when faced with a hundred-dollar tank of gas and the forecasted depletion of the earth's petroleum, wondered if there was a better use of their money. Annie Leonard's 2007 documentary film, *The Story of Stuff*, voiced anticonsumerist ideas in language and cartoons so unthreatening that it has been played to countless school groups, translated into fifteen languages, and viewed by 12 million people.

Those still unconvinced that our freewheeling system of commerce had led us astray were stirred to outrage in 2008. When the dust of the subprime mortgage derby settled, we learned that the captains of finance had bet the neighbor's farm on Endless Boom, but hedged with a personal wager on Inevitable Bust. The fortunes of financiers survived intact while middle-class investors and working-class pensioners were left with a pocketful of stubs. By 2010, the income gap was more severe than ever, with 1 percent of Americans owning 24 percent of the wealth, up from 18 percent in 1915. "Economically speaking, the richest nation on earth is starting to resemble a banana republic," Timothy Noah wrote in *Slate*. Ten years after koala's call to arms against the "all-oppressive dollar," no less staid a publication than *The New Yorker* conceded, "Much of what investment bankers do is socially worthless."

But what could a concerned citizen do? Upset as I was about a drift of plastic the size of Texas swirling at sea, I was mired in my own web of noxious entanglements. I wasn't going to go live in a cave about it. But selectively opting out of the money system isn't easy: if you're in for a dime, you're in for a dollar. Like many Americans, I am upset that the government seizes a portion of my income to squander on purposes I regard as immoral. For me, the sticking point is the war in Iraq; for others it might be publicly funded abortions or teaching Darwin in public schools. I deployed my legal means of democratic participation—voting, writing letters to Congress, walking in peaceful protest—without result. I resolved to withhold federal income tax, even ready, like Thoreau, to spend a night in jail. But consequences for such civil disobedience have increased by Draconian orders of magnitude since the 1840s: instead of a sleepover in the village clink, Uncle Sam would confiscate my home, fine me one hundred grand, and lock me in prison for five years. This was a sacrifice I was unwilling to make. Regardless of who I voted for, or what slogans I affixed to my bumper, if I paid taxes, I was a supporter of the war. Many people feel this powerlessness in their search for a simple, moral life this side of the wilderness and the jail.

It's possible to compromise. The gamut of those who take to heart the concept of living simply is wider than Suelo and the freegans, and it's crammed with people who don't want to boycott everything; they just want to buy less junk and do less harm. As the Center for the New American Dream encouraged people to "work less, live more, and consume more consciously," a Prius-driving cousin of freeganism emerged, spouting catchphrases like "postconsumer" and "cradle to cradle." These were less the spawn of Abbie Hoffman than of Helen and Scott Nearing, whose 1954 book *Living the Good Life* inspired the back-to-the-land movement of the 1970s. Some celebrated Buy Nothing Day, a counterweight to the buying frenzy that occurs the day after Thanksgiving that has become almost a holiday in its own right. The Freecycle Network, which champions a "gift economy" of giving away used items rather than sending them to the landfill, claims more than eight million members. Couchsurfing.com built a worldwide network of hosts and travelers who stay for free in one another's homes. New books contributed not so much shrill warnings that we'd acquired too much, but practical visions for surviving with less: *Deep Economy: The Wealth of Communities and the Durable Future; Simple Prosperity: Finding Real Wealth in a Sustainable Lifestyle;* and *Plenitude: The New Economics of True Wealth.*

Thermostats were adjusted, tires properly inflated, trees planted, lightbulbs replaced. I took my own steps toward withholding money from industries I didn't want to support: I pedaled my bike instead of driving, I installed a high-efficiency furnace, I closed my account at a national bank and transferred the money to a local credit union. That plastic drift in the Pacific came to represent for me all that was wrong: thoughtless use of disposable products, profit-driven mass manufacture of toxic goods, our inability to pick up our trash, technological innovation that had created problems beyond our ability to fix them. I began to reuse Ziplocs and carry cloth bags to the grocery market.

But here was the problem: although these actions made sense, they didn't make me feel any less anxious, or more free. How many times have I stood at the kitchen sink paralyzed by a plastic baggie? If it were clean, having held, say, a sandwich, I'd simply rinse and reuse it. But this one is smeared with mustard and rancid cheese and even a bit of mold. My instinct is to throw it away. But as we have learned, there is no such place as "away." This plastic bag, if it doesn't end up clogging the intestines of some albatross or dolphin, will swirl at sea for decades, and even after it breaks down into tiny pieces, it will never fully decompose: its toxic petrochemicals will haunt us forever.

But then I think: *That's ridiculous. It's just one baggie. And the washing of it will not only be a singularly unpleasant use of my time, but won't I be using precious water to wash it? And burning natural gas to heat that water. Not to mention the resource depletion and damage represented by the soap.* And by now I've already wasted five minutes thinking about this, time that could have been better spent picking up plastic bags along the river.

So I chuck the thing in the trash, but the next day at breakfast it's still there, peering up at me accusingly. And the gears of my mind spin. Eventually, one day in the future, I'm going to need a plastic sandwich baggie. And when I do, I'm going to buy a box of them, thus giving my hard-earned money to the Ziploc corporation, or whoever, who doubtlessly engages in all sorts of toxic practices to manufacture these things—I imagine a factory spewing brown sludge into a river, somewhere in the Rust Belt, or maybe China. And I'll also be enabling my box of baggies to be hauled across the nation on gas-guzzling trucks that grind up the taxpayer-funded highways, which carve through the habitat of grizzlies and moose and antelope, driving them toward extinction, and so on.

Finally I had to ask a therapist about this, and he said, "Why don't you try going outside and growing something?"

I signed up to volunteer at a community garden not far from my house, and spent two afternoons per week pulling weeds, spreading mulch, picking cucumbers. I worked alongside strangers. They became friends. I had a better idea of what was happening in my own town. My back ached and I was glad about it. The fresh food was a boon (although I'm still not sure what to do with bok choy), and I felt good knowing they arrived on my plate without the use of chemical fertilizers or interstate trucking or exploited migrants. But what I really liked was to be outside, physically *doing* something with other people. Unlike washing (or not washing) plastic bags, growing food made me feel good.

Little did I know, I'd stumbled into the most vibrant wing

of voluntary simplicity: the local food movement. In the past decade there has been a blossoming of homegrown produce, community shared agriculture, volunteer gardens, and farmers' markets. Although the trend had percolated through the grassroots since the eighties, its jump to the mainstream coincided with recent economic and environmental calamities. Eric Schlosser's 2001 *Fast Food Nation* exposed the moral costs and health hazards of cheap eats, and caused many to change their habits. Michael Pollan turned the heretofore soporific topic of food production and distribution into a 2007 best-selling page-turner, *The Omnivore's Dilemma*, which along with Barbara Kingsolver's *Animal, Vegetable, Miracle* celebrated what was by then a national tide of local sustainable farming.

Chris Conrad's Sol Food Farms, where Suelo was a regular volunteer, typifies this movement. Like Free Meal, its reason for being is loftier than to merely provide food. The word "economy," Chris Conrad told me, comes from the Greek terms for "home" and "management." In other words, it means "taking care of your home." The Greeks were largely an agrarian society, he said, so one could interpret their economy as "people who properly manage their homeland." Grassroots operations like Sol Foods could provide a new template for the way humans steward the land.

However, when I visited, the idealistic operation had yet to turn a profit. In its first summer Chris had ended up giving away surplus crops. I asked if he wasn't worried about financial security.

"Spinach," Chris Conrad said. "That's my retirement. I've always been interested in self-sufficiency, and I like knowing I'll always have my own food."

When I still didn't see how this was going to translate to a salary, he clarified that his business plan was based largely on a new economy that would emerge "after the collapse." In the era of peak oil, the belief has become widespread that our current system of trucking food from California and Iowa, or flying it in from Peru, is simply doomed. "Imagine if semi trucks can't get into City Market because we've run out of fossil fuels," Brer Erschadi told me, referring to a local grocery store. "This town will clear off the shelves in a matter of days. Then what?"

Chris Conrad is not quite so apocalyptic, but he does mention that his irrigation system, the old gravity-fed ditches carved by settlers over a century ago, could function just fine without electricity. He anticipates not only the failure of the fossil-fuel grid, but also the collapse of the monetary system. "We even issued our own currency," he told me. He printed "Sun Dollars," which exchanged at a one-to-one rate with United States dollars. Sun Dollars could be redeemed at the farmers' market for produce or burritos or whatever Chris was making that day. It was a clever ploy to get folks to prepay, but Conrad sees deeper implications. "After the collapse, one Sun Dollar might be worth two green dollars, so you'd be smart to hold on to them."

"But what if the collapse doesn't happen?" I said. "Or what if it takes twenty years?"

He'd considered this. "Maybe it will just be the rich hippies who buy my produce and pay my mortgage. And I guess I'm fine with that."

The most pressing concern, meanwhile, is merely keeping the crops in the soil. As most utopias have learned, idealists don't always make the best laborers. Ultimately, a volunteer like Suelo didn't really care whether or not Sol Food delivered its vegetables to market and turned a profit. By the end of summer, he was more interested in harvesting feral crops like rye that had sprung up on the farm's periphery—he said it was more in line with his hunting-and-gathering ethos.

And farming is a fickle business, not like a lot of modern jobs where you get paid just to show up. That day I worked in the orchard, the wind picked up. The willows leaned hard, and an acre of cottonwood leaves that had been spread as mulch sailed into the sky. Chris Conrad grimaced. "We need to get that stuff tilled before we lose it all." Still the gales increased. Sheets of corrugated tin from a nearby construction site soared into the air and rolled across the fields. Dust and leaves and thorns batted against us. "The gods are angry with us!" Suelo called, tumbleweeds swirling overhead.

And then, the hoop house, a prized ten-by-thirty-foot growing structure, lifted off the ground, backflipped violently over the deer fence, and crashed down on top of Chris Conrad's truck. "It's times like this I'm glad I'm just a volunteer," said Brer.

Indeed, after a second year in the red, Chris Conrad ended the commercial venture. He told me that he'd still be growing food for his own larder, but he wasn't sure if or when he'd go back into business. Sun Dollars, however, would still be valid. "If you have Sun Dollars you'd like to spend, please contact me," he wrote on his website. "I continue to believe that local currencies (like Sun Dollars) will surpass the value of the US Dollar in the near future."

Free Meal suffered a similar fate. In 2011, after August Brooks couldn't find someone else to offer a kitchen, the program was indefinitely suspended. The problem with utopias is that they rely almost entirely on the commitment of their founders—a sure recipe for burnout.

Such setbacks notwithstanding, Sol Food Farms and Free

Meal and projects like them all across the country are changing the way we grow and distribute food. They are cutting the amount of chemicals and fossil fuels in the food system, and reducing what gets thrown away—two considerable feats. They may never counteract the seemingly apocalyptic conditions that necessitate their existence in the first place—they are up against global warming and a monetary system rigged in favor of bankers, and how many tons of tomatoes will unpaid philosophers have to grow to reverse that?—but as I learned at the garden where I volunteered, it ain't about the tomatoes.

Maybe the process of trying to change the world is as valuable as actually attaining that change. Because what's gained is a renewed sense of community, of knowing your neighbor. And ultimately, building community may solve problems like excessive consumption that result from Americans' extreme version of individuality.

In the final months of Free Meal, August Brooks got a glimpse of how something as simple as free food could break down barriers between social classes. But he soon encountered a hard fact of activism: it's easier to give away food than to change people's hearts. After all, building community forces people to confront the fears and judgments that caused them to withdraw from community in the first place. One of my most idealistic female friends aborted her maiden voyage to Free Meal when, before she even exited her vehicle, a drunk bum solicited a cigarette and her phone number. I had my own qualms. After a half-dozen lunches accompanied by conspiratorial rants among the regulars—"Rich people want a nuclear war, that's why they've all built private bunkers"—I found myself thinking, in defiance of my progressive inclinations, *Why don't you people get a job?*

"People say, 'I want to support what you're doing,' and they want to give money or donate food," August Brooks says. "I tell them the best thing they can do is come down and eat with us. But most of them never do. They're afraid of the stigma of getting a handout, and also they're uncomfortable to mix with what they perceive are poor people."

Which is all a way of saying: this whole project of changing the world is hard work. And as much as we seek a balance, straddling the line between individualism and community isn't a recipe for freedom. It's the opposite. When you try to balance the anxiety of maintaining wealth (savings, mortgages, insurance) with the anxiety of being an ethical person (eating local food, lunching with hobos, reusing baggies, withholding taxes), you don't free yourself from either. You end up with twice the anxiety. It's sort of like going on a diet. Unless you're willing to go all in—run six miles a day and eat only fish and broccoli—you'll never have those sculpted abs you see in magazines. But neither will you have the unabashed joy of scarfing double-frosted chocolate cake. Instead you nibble away at half a piece, your enjoyment negated by your guilt that you couldn't refuse it altogether.

The person with the least worry over the compromises he must make is, of course, the person who doesn't compromise: Suelo. "Before, my hardships were long-term, complex anxieties," he says: "What am I going to do with my life, how am I going to pay rent or pay insurance, what's retirement going to be like, what am I going to do for a career, what are people going to think if I do this or that? To me that stuff is actually unbearable. And I think most people are dealing with it. Now my hardships are simple and immediate: food, shelter, and clothing. They're manageable because they're in the present."

The most important result of his quitting money, then, is not a reduction of carbon emissions, or a lasting protest against the money system, but drawing a map to the freedom that lies within every person's grasp, even if we never choose to pursue it. Unlike the rest of us, Suelo is unaffected by the chaos of the markets. In the twelve years since he quit money, while the economy has convulsed, his life has not changed much. Amid travels, volunteering, and friendships, he's achieved a sort of stasis. The drama of his path from faith to despair and back, which dominated twenty years of his life, more or less ended when he stopped using money. He seems to have lost track of the years, which may be a product of middle-aged absentmindedness, but I'd attribute it to his genuine success at escaping a linear model of time.

"I don't expect everybody to live in a cave and dumpster-dive," he says. "I do implore everybody to take only what they know in their own hearts that they need, and give up excess to those who have less than they need. If this happened, I certainly wouldn't have to dumpster-dive."

Suelo was unfazed by the downfall of the community groups he supported. The next year, he helped launch a program to grow vegetables in people's untended lawns, and give away the harvest. He still volunteers with the Youth Garden Project, which despite the economic downturn continues to expand. Attracting a new crop of AmeriCorps members each year, the farm not only grows food and runs a weekly market, but also operates high school science classes, an after-school program for kids, a summer day camp, and court-ordered community service for juvenile offenders—not to mention playing host to the nation's premier pumpkin-catapulting event.

I spent an evening there with Suelo and a young crew who

believed they could improve the world one carrot at a time. We pulled weeds in the golden shade of cottonwoods, by a creek pouring down from the mountains. As we gathered for a feast of beans and squash and greens and peppers that were harvested within a hundred yards of where we sat, I believed in their dream, too.

"I do envision money going obsolete," says Suelo. "I envision communal living, making it possible for families to live moneyless. Communal living already exists in every society, even here in the most capitalistic. It's called sharing, what we learn in kindergarten. We must cultivate it until it chokes out our selfish system naturally."

14

. . .

To die but not to perish is to be eternally present.

—Lao-tzu

ON A SUMMER day Suelo and I drove up the winding road to Mount Evans. I wanted to see the spot where he drove off the cliff.

His survival has the trappings of a miracle. His last thought, as he floored the accelerator, was that if God had some purpose for his life, He wouldn't allow it to end like this. As Suelo blacked out, the car soared off the road, tumbled along the rocks, then ground to a halt on a steep patch of grass, teetering over the abyss. He woke up. Everything was red. Shattered glass. A curtain of blood over his eyes. *Oh shit, I'm still alive.* He didn't feel any pain. *Well, there's no way I could have survived that,* he reasoned, and drifted off. He felt comfortable, sleepy. Soon it would be over.

He awoke again. He was shivering. It was a cold spring dawn and the temperature was just above freezing. He would die soon.

His survival instinct overwhelmed his death wish. *I don't want to die!* he thought. *I gotta get up to the road.* He blacked out again.

The next time he awoke, he was lying on the side of the road. He heard an engine above: someone was driving down the mountain. A man covered Suelo with a blanket, then sped down the hill to find a phone. The next thing Suelo remembers was being loaded into a helicopter.

When I asked Daniel's mother how she explained her son's survival, she was quick with Scripture. "If you make the Lord your refuge, he will give his angels charge of you, and in their hands they will bear you up," promises the Book of Psalms. But Suelo himself is not a believer in miracles. He doesn't know exactly how he found his way out of the wreck and up to the road, but he doesn't purport to have been carried by angels. He does not claim to be a saint or prophet, or to have a direct line with God. Even his breakthrough night of meditation in Thailand he considers to have been a moment of profound truth—no more, no less. When I asked him if he thought that he had attained enlightenment, he said no. He thinks enlightenment is a continual process, one that he struggles toward daily. What's more, Suelo doesn't consider himself a seer, like Hindu mystics or Indian shamans.

"I like to spend long times meditating and fasting, but I wouldn't say I have visions," he says. "We think there is something better in another realm, but the purpose of this lifestyle is to live in the here and now. There is no need for the otherworldly visions."

His goal—his journey—has been simply to live as much as possible like the great religious figures: Jesus, Buddha, Mohammed, Lao-tzu. But he never claims to *be* like them.

An evangelical Christian once snorted to Suelo, "What, you think you can live like Jesus?"

"Well, don't you?" Suelo replied.

The exchange illustrates Suelo's beef with organized religion: "Wasn't that what Jesus said: do what I do? He was here as an example for us to follow. Same with all prophets. Didn't the prophets tell us to be like them? That's what's wrong with Christianity. They make Jesus and the prophets into icons, take them off of earth, and put them in heaven to worship them, so they're no longer accessible. You've taken a reality and made it into a worthless idol. Christians talk about the idolatry of other religions, but when they no longer live principles and just worship the people who taught them, that's exactly what they're doing."

For all his pantheistic exploring and complaints about fundamentalism, however, Suelo remains close to—and in a sense truest to—the values with which he was raised. His family still lives those values, too. After his brother died in 1994, the Shellabargers quit Motel 6 and moved to Fruita, to be closer to Rick's widow and their grandson. They were approaching seventy, without significant income or retirement funds. That's when Dick's brother Les—he of Shellabarger Chevrolet—intervened. He built a new house and moved them in, said they could live there rent-free as long as they wished. The Shellabargers still teach Bible study classes in their home. They invite indigent people—drug addicts, victims of abuse—to stay with them.

When Suelo and I drove the hundred miles from Moab to visit them, he brought unopened packages of eggs and cheese and bacon from a dumpster and prepared breakfast. While he cooked, Laurel showed me framed paintings that Daniel had completed over the years. A few days before my visit, she had emailed me a cordial invitation, adding, "We have some things we would like to show you that Daniel has done in the past and that mean so much to us." One of the things Mrs. Shellabarger wanted to show me, as I presently learned, was a handmade booklet of passages from the Book of Proverbs, each accompanied by a watercolor depicting scenes of nature that Daniel had completed in high school. Another was a cloudy gray painting of ducks on a pond that Daniel gave them as a gift a decade later. "It's a sad-looking picture," said Dick, "because of his brother dying, see, when he done that."

Despite the warm welcome, I was surprised by their acceptance of—actually, pride in—Daniel for the life he leads.

"He's his own man," said Dick. "I'm proud because he's doing what he wants to do."

I couldn't help but see the similarity between Daniel and his father. Both are the youngest in big families, with older brothers more successful with careers and finances. Both refused to work jobs where they felt exploited. Both are extreme in their religious views, taking literally what many dismiss as metaphor, and both are prone to deep exploration of Scripture, and to fierce debates about what it says and means—debates for which the mainstream cares little. Both have lived rent-free by the generosity of others.

Indeed, most of the Shellabargers' quarrels with their son are strictly theological, disagreements over biblical interpretation that to non-Christians might seem mere hairsplitting. "Daniel's taken the Bible and spiritualized it," Dick said. "For instance, he says that the Kingdom of Heaven is now, that Christ has returned spiritually, and there will be no physical return. We have crossed swords on it, but we decided we love each other too much to fight." Dick Shellabarger also takes issue with Daniel's universalism. "He's mixed up with all these cults and false religions, see? Islam, Buddhism, Hinduism. He gets with these false religions and he goes haywire. Some of the emails he writes are really in left field. Christianity is being run down because we're narrow-minded—but we are the only way."

Like his parents, Daniel's siblings have remained traditional Christians, and they, too, take to heart the priorities they grew up with. None of them is wealthy. After raising eight children, Pennie and her husband got a divorce, and she recently remarried. Rick's widow, Elaine, is raising her son alone in a modest home a few blocks from the Shellabargers. Ron is disabled and lives nearby in an assisted-living facility. Doug, who holds a master's degree in counseling, suffered a spinal injury in a car accident and was unable to work for two years, after which he lost his job as a psychotherapist, and his wife divorced him. Now he works at Home Depot.

I asked Elaine if she was embarrassed by Daniel's life.

"No," she said. "The family does disagree with some points. We think he's too extreme, but he's fighting against greed, self-sufficiency, and impersonalness. If he moved two steps closer, we'd agree. Greed and pride are the two primary problems in America, and this current economy shows that greed is the worst." When I asked Ron what he thought of his kid brother's life, he grinned and said, "It's totally cool."

Doug, just fifteen months older, is closest to Daniel, especially after his own misfortunes forced him to rethink money and the decisions he had assumed would bring wealth. "The paths we've taken diverged—but didn't. That's the paradox," Doug told me, smoking a pipe on the deck of his converted cabin in the mountains near Denver, not too far from the site of his grandparents' dude ranch. "There really is a benefit when you come into contact with Dan, even if you don't share his beliefs. He gives, and expects absolutely nothing in return."

And yet there remains Daniel's sexuality, an area of his life about which his family maintains willful ignorance. Having a gay son continues to both vex and edify the Shellabargers.

"I don't know if he's ever had sexual contact," said Laurel. "You have to remain celibate. It's not a sin if you don't act on it. But Jesus also said if you commit adultery in your heart, that's a sin."

Now we sat there wondering: *Well, is it a sin, or isn't it?* Finally Dick ended the stalemate.

"Being gay is a defect in the brain, just like my other son who has cerebral palsy," he proposed. "But I can't throw them both out because they have defects. I love them all the more."

"But are you worried he'll end up in hell?" I asked the Shellabargers.

"He's accepted Christ as his savior," Laurel said.

"When was that?"

"When he was seven."

After years of trying to convince them that his being gay was no aberration, Daniel accepted a sort of detente: his family assumes that he is asexual and he doesn't tell them differently. Still, isn't it painful to have his family view him as a eunuch?

"I don't necessarily disagree with it," Suelo says. "My

philosophy of life is that everything is true on some level. And besides, I've never been a particularly sexual person. As far as explaining everything in biblical terms, they do that with everything and everybody. That's how they resolve things, find harmony. In that way I felt like my coming-out was a good thing for them. It gave them a koan to see how this fits."

Dick was working behind the counter of a Christian bookstore when a gay man came in to browse for books. The two struck up a conversation. Dick mentioned that his son was gay, and the man teared up, telling him how as a gay man he could find no Christian fellowship in Grand Junction.

"I said: 'God loves you as much as he loves me,'" remembers Dick. "He was so thankful. We talked for hours, after the store had closed. The man told me, 'I have enjoyed this more than anything in my life.' "

I remembered something Suelo had told me about his parents. As a young man, he'd resented their unshakable faith, and thought they were blind and narrow-minded. But with age he has come to appreciate it. "It's allowed them to maintain such a pure, almost childlike innocence," he told me, "which is a beautiful way of seeing the world."

One of his lessons has been that the religion that rejects him also gave him a lot. "We all have roots, and if we cut them off we die," he says. "There were priceless things in my upbringing I needed to reconcile with. I was an ingrate for not acknowledging all the good that was given to me freely. When I reconnect with old friends, they say we'd love to go to your house because it was such a loving family, while theirs were fighting all the time, and alcoholism. I was realizing that every family on this planet is fucked up in some way or another. I'd been focusing on the negative parts of my own, and not seeing the good parts. My parents always loved each other, and didn't fight, weren't abusive."

Just as Suelo can admire his parents as they reject his sexuality, so can he reject the bigotry of their brand of Christianity while embracing its potential for personal and societal transformation. "So I somehow have to learn to take the good and leave the bad, remembering the things that were valid and profound with what I was raised with, and getting rid of the narrow-mindedness and hypocrisy."

Brian Mahan, Daniel's CU professor, sees his former student's spiritual path not merely as a route to personal holiness, but as a deeply moral act. Now a scholar-in-residence at the Union Theological Seminary in New York, Mahan is an expert on William James and the author of *Forgetting Ourselves on Purpose: Vocation and the Ethics of Ambition,* a meditation on the choices between worldly success and a meaningful spiritual life. He told me that Daniel's was the sort of moral choice—albeit far more drastic—that he had encouraged students to make. The topic still preoccupies him. Dr. Mahan writes: "Poverty is indeed the strenuous life, James writes, without brass bands or hysteric popular applause or lies or circumlocutions, and when one sees the way in which wealth-getting enters as an ideal into the very bone and marrow of our generation, one wonders whether the revival of the belief that poverty is a worthy religious vocation may not be the transformation of military courage, and the spiritual reform which our time stands most in need of."

I asked Mahan if he felt responsible for Daniel's way of life. Had he filled a young student's head with lofty ideas about giving up ambition and money, not meaning them to be taken so literally?

"I'm actually embarrassed that Daniel is so much more intentional about it than me!" he said with a laugh. "I never envisioned anyone being quite that radical." More soberly, he reflected, "It is for all of us to answer, why we question the Dans in the world."

.   .   .

As Daniel and I drove up Mount Evans, we encountered a bicycle race to its summit. Car traffic crawled behind the cyclists. We pulled off to wait for the traffic to thin. Fifteen minutes later we resumed driving. We figured we'd catch the line of vehicles soon, but after five miles we still hadn't seen another car.

"Maybe they all decided to drive off the cliff," Suelo said.

Suelo will admit that he's never totally outgrown the evangelical streak instilled in him by his parents. He thinks others will benefit from what he has learned, so he doesn't hesitate to talk about it. "Is it a bad thing to want to change someone? Is just talking to someone an influence? Should I zip my mouth and not speak?"

Moreover, he's come to recognize the power of belief to effect change, even if no one religion has a monopoly on the truth. By studying Gandhi and Martin Luther King, he believes that the most effective social movements are those with a spiritual center. "It took me years to get beyond my antagonism against religion, which appears more destructive than constructive, until I saw at its core the paradox, the power of change, like a Trojan horse within the walls of commercial civilization," he says.

Wherever they are and whatever they believe, Suelo tries to reach the people he thinks really need his message. It can be a tricky balancing act. Secular leftists are attracted to his moneyless message; they already despise banks and corporations, and believe that greed is the root of most of the world's problems. But they are generally not receptive to religious overtures. Suelo gets along just fine with freegan anarchists in the streets of Portland—until he drops the J-bomb. Broadly speaking, punk-rockers think Christianity is the problem, not the solution.

"When I'm up in Portland, people don't understand that rural America is fundamentalist," he says. "There's a whole population of Americans that won't budge an inch unless we speak their language. That's why I've chosen to stick with religious language."

Take a look at the comments on Suelo's blog, and you'll see what he means. Most of his harshest critics are fundamentalists, quoting Scripture in their attempts to convince Suelo to repent and return to the flock. Suelo, of course, can quote Scripture right back at them.

"When I was a kid I thought I'd be a missionary to the heathens, but now I think maybe it's okay to be a missionary, but to the Christians, because they're the ones who need it, because they don't believe their own religion."

By that, he means that most devout Christians have become so obsessed with theology—with Jesus's Second Coming and with preparing their souls for the afterlife—that they've stopped following His most basic teachings about loving your enemy, turning the other cheek, and blessing the meek. He thinks his path might illuminate the way for dissatisfied Christians.

"I decided to walk away from fundamentalism, even with the threat of eternal hell looming over my head," he wrote in a 2010 comment thread, debating some readers. "Walking away from the vise-grip of fundamentalism isn't easy, so, please, you non-fundamentalists, have compassion on fundamentalists. I went through years of intense depression.

"Then I found my liberation. I resigned myself to hell. Yes. I decided I'd rather be in hell with Gandhi, Martin Luther King, Vivekananda, Ramakrishna, Mother Teresa, Buddha, Kabir, Rumi, Peace Pilgrim and, yes, with Jesus Himself, than to be in heaven with the torturous fundamentalist mentality that thinks itself right and everybody else wrong. I decided I'd rather be in hell for love than to be in heaven for bigotry."

Suelo's ultimate goal is not to change a policy or repeal a law, but to live his beliefs. He found the material world a living hell, and when he tried to end his life, he was given the opportunity to start over, and live a spiritual life instead.

High up on the road to the summit of Mount Evans, we found a tiny pullout and parked. We descended the steep slope to the site of Daniel's wreck. Twenty years had passed, and though he had returned to the site a few years afterward, he now had some trouble identifying the exact spot. It was midsummer, but the flanks of the mountain were wrapped in cold cloud. We squeezed between white granite blocks, climbing with our hands over boulders, all the while eyeing the green lake far below. A patch of gray snow shivered in the ravine. Yellow and white wildflowers dotted the slope, along with bunches of grass with purple buds, and tufts of spiny-leaved plants.

"Nettles," Daniel said. "You can eat those."

We surveyed the narrow ledges of grass between the cliff bands. The air was thin and cold. Our breaths were quick. At fifty, Suelo found himself nervous at such exposed heights. Merely walking along the cliff frightened him, to say nothing of trying to drive a car off it. "What the fuck was I thinking?" he said.

I asked him how he interpreted his miraculous survival.

"I finally felt the hand of God," he said with a laugh. "And I hated it."

If God did intervene—if Suelo did survive the crash for a reason—then it wasn't the act of a sentimental God who wanted to prevent grief and suffering. The God Suelo believes in carried him up that cliff to put him to work, to dare him to align his actions with his faith, to force him to build heaven where he saw only hell.

We weren't sure if we had found the ledge. We were hoping for some broken glass, a hubcap—something to prove we were in the right place. But after narrowing it down to two benches, we called it good and ascended the scree toward the road, mounting fridge-sized rocks that wobbled beneath our shoes.

"It seems we have free will, but we don't," said Suelo. "It isn't my choice whether I live or die."

And that's where I like to leave Suelo—on the flank of the mountain, climbing that cliff, with or without his free will, striving to find a life worth living. As one philosopher said of the hero Sisyphus and his eternal task of pushing a boulder up a mountain, the struggle toward the heights is itself enough to fill a man's heart. If God had a purpose for Suelo, then even Suelo could not resist it. Daniel Shellabarger died as modern man driving his car over a cliff, and was reborn as eternal man—without money or possessions, with only his two feet and two hands, trying to climb back to the top. "And where we thought to find an abomination, we shall find a god," writes Joseph Campbell. "Where we had thought to slay another, we shall slay ourselves; where we had thought to travel outward, we shall come to the center of our own existence; where we had thought to be alone, we shall be with the world."

The struggle itself toward the eternal present is enough to fill a man's heart. One must imagine Suelo happy.

ACKNOWLEDGMENTS

First, I am grateful to Daniel Suelo, who gave me his story freely, in all senses. When Becky Saletan at Riverhead Books first contacted him to gauge his interest in a book, he wrote, "I, of course, couldn't take a penny or anything else for it, otherwise it would render the whole thing nonsense." From the outset of the time we worked together, Daniel said that he would withhold nothing, and I believe he kept that promise. He opened his heart, and encouraged the same of his family and friends, who not only answered my questions but often fed me and gave me a place to sleep. I feel especially thankful for getting to know the Shellabarger family: Richard and Laurel, Doug, Ron and Elaine. I must single out the contributions of Tim Frederick, Timothy Wojtusik, and Damian Nash, who handed over troves of Daniel's personal letters (with his permission) that recaptured so many lost years. Irv Thomas also sent an archive of old emails.

Acknowledgments

I'd like to thank Conrad Sorenson for lending his rich story to
this book.

My friends and neighbors in Moab were invaluable in depict-
ing the town's personality and charting Suelo's path through it.
They are: Chris Conrad, August Brooks, Andrew Riley, Dorina
Krusemer, Linda Whitham, Bill Hedden, Frankling Seal, Brer
Erschadi, Rayburn Price, Roberta Ossana, Whitney Rearick,
Pete Gross. Special thanks to the ladies of the Youth Garden
Project: Jen Sadoff, Rhonda Gotway, and Delite Primus. Criti-
cal to piecing together Suelo's eventful life story were Dawn
Larson, Rebecca Mullen, Corinne Pochitaloff, Brian Mahan,
Michael Friedman, Randy Kinkel, Kathryn Chindaporn, Satya
Vatu, Mel Scully, Ander Olaizola, Tre Arrow, James Ward, Sam
Harmon, Logan White, Roy Ramirez, Phillip Maughmer.

It is a truism to say that a book does not come into existence
by the mere toil of its author, but nonetheless, the product you
hold in your hands is evidence that it takes a village to make a
sausage. I am grateful to the writer Christopher Ketchum, without whose fine magazine story on Suelo this book might never
have been born. Blaine Honea sent me a Student Bible, which
I finally read. Isan Brant contributed the author photo to the
cause. Barb and Scott Brant welcomed me to their family and
taught me things about faith that I believe will outlast my writing of this volume.

The first people to get an inkling of what I was up to were
my students and colleagues in the MFA writing program at
Western Connecticut State University, who listened to me read
the very first draft in a microphone in a hotel bar in Danbury.
Their barrage of questions and loud dissent indicated I was on
to something good. I'd like to thank Brian Clements, who for

six years flew me from Montana to teach there, and my fellow writers-in-residence—Paola Corso, Elizabeth Cohen, Dan Pope, Daniel Asa Rose, and Don Snyder. I am also grateful to Sharon Oard Warner and Greg Martin at the University of New Mexico for repeatedly welcoming me back to the Taos Summer Writers Conference.

The people at Riverhead/Penguin not only made this book much better than it otherwise might have been, but revealed enough true enthusiasm for the project to convince me it was a good idea. I am grateful to Elaine Trevorrow, Martin Karlow, Pamela Barricklow, Tamara Arellano, Ashley Fisher-Tranese, Rick Pascocello, Liz Psaltis, Alex Merto, Tiffany Estreicher, Helen Yentus, Caitlin Mulrooney-Lyski, and Craig Burke. Melissa Kahn at 3 Arts Entertainment kept the train on the rails.

I was guided intellectually and aesthetically and emotionally through the writing of this book—as with previous books—by my dear friends Melony Gilles and Mathew Gross, worthy companions for both metaphysical inquiry and whitewater beer drinking.

The earliest readers of this book were Richard and Rosemary Sundeen, former seminarians both, whose breadth of religious and academic know-how made them ideal sounding boards, not to mention fine parents. The manuscript benefitted from the rigorous line edits of Ellen Finnigan ("Poor Mark!"), Elizabeth Hightower Allen ("yeah yeah yeah"), and Erik Bluhm ("It's Pat!"). I'd also like to thank for reading early drafts and chapters: my brother Rich Sundeen, Stan and Sharon Bluhm, Tim Bluhm, Eric Puchner, Antonya Nelson, Leslie Howes, Ashley Gallagher, and Alissa Johnson.

My agent Richard Abate has stuck with me for more than a

decade. His intellect, loyalty, and friendship debunks the things we provincials are led to believe about New York literary agents. Publisher Geoffrey Kloske deserves credit for more than once unwisely gambling his otherwise good name on me. In an era when book editors are widely assumed to speak only the language of sales charts, tie-ins, and platforms, Becky Saletan showed what perhaps it was like, way back when, when editors brought as much passion and curiosity and creativity as did the authors. In a year filled with trials she returned to this manuscript again and again with insight and care. I am grateful.

Cedar Brant applied the ear of a poet and the wisdom of a pilgrim. Over the course of writing this book she also helped me bury Sadie my dingo, threw me a fortieth birthday party, and agreed to marry me. Love love love.